LOVELY DISASTER

ERIN HUNT

LANDON
HAIL
PRESS

Paperback ISBN: 978-1-959955-04-7
Hardback ISBN: 978-1-959955-08-5

Published by Landon Hail Press
Cover design and cover/author photos by Andy Petek
Cover shoot styled by Samantha Joy

Disclaimer: This work depicts actual events in the life of the author as truthfully as recollection permits and/or can be verified by research. Occasionally, dialogue consistent with the character or nature of the person speaking has been supplemented. All persons within are actual individuals; there are no composite characters. The names of some individuals have been changed to respect their privacy.

"To love oneself is the beginning of a lifelong romance."

—Oscar Wilde

CONTENTS

Prologue 7

August 19, 2017 10

August 20, 2017: Buellton, California 12

August 21, 2017: Denver, Colorado 13

August 22, 2017 15

1990 18

August 22, 2017 20

Being Uncomfortable 26

England 34

The Hustle 48

Temptation 54

Religion 58

The Layers in our Eyes 69

Loss 76

My Grandfather 81

Partying 87

Sex 104

Crime and Punishment 117

Adventures 143

Friendships 150

The Con 159

Resign as Peacekeeping Envoy! 169

Health 175

Moab Mishaps 196

Acknowledgments 201

About the Author 207

Prologue

Can you remember when something changed you? Not changed like a hair color or a new diet or a new job. But when your footing fell away, when the bile rose in your throat, and you had an immediate memory that would never, ever leave you? When everything in your life, instead of seeming to pass you by, was instead placed before you like a gluttonous five-course meal? When you looked in the mirror and didn't recognize yourself anymore, or anyone else for that matter?

There have been a few for me. Some felt devastating and tragic. Some felt like magical "pinch-me" moments. And then there are some that seemed mundane and average at the time but turned out to be utter emotional earthquakes.

For me, my moment took place in my favorite restaurant, eating my favorite salad, drinking a bottle of Sancerre, and having a wonderful night of deep, thoughtful, and sincere conversations with a friend whom I cannot explain how much I treasure. While I tend to be quite pragmatic when it comes to friendships, I usually do not describe mine in such context. But this night, this friend, and our conversation swallowed me up and changed my own trajectory. At forty-seven, I have learned how utterly important these kinds of relationships and friendships are. I have now deliberately built them into my DNA, my biological makeup, because without them, I truly and vulnerably admit I do not believe I would be alive today.

We split a salad. We caught up on life. We checked in with each other, as we always do. We talked about our kids, our lives, our homes, our husbands. And we laughed. We laughed until it hurt. We reminisced about our crazy escapades in the past, our utter heartbreaks in the last few years, and we both agreed how unreal it felt to be where we are now. For longer than I care to admit, this comfortable place felt unfathomable. To us both, I believe, to be honest. I recalled a dinner with her years before wherein my poise and grace had been smothered or, rather, flushed down the toilet as I spoke my truth to her, fraught with tears, fear, and shame.

And I can still remember hearing her say back to me, "You are not alone. We are doing this together. And whatever you choose, I love you and will always support you."

On this particular night, over our salads and Sancerre, we talked about how we could write a "manual" based on our experiences. And that was it. The switch was flipped and couldn't be turned off. Thoughts, memories, and people swirled around in my head for months after that, and I realized I'd started something in my head and heart that I had to release. And so, this book was born.

So, to you, my dear friend, and to all of my friends who have kept me safe and have held me in their hearts, never judging me or belittling me when I fall, my gratitude doesn't even cover it. I hope whoever is reading this has these kinds of people in your corner, who recognize when you need more care and love from them than you can give back in return. Those who cheer on your accomplishments without fail or question. And if you ever doubt whether you have people like that around you, or if you doubt who is on your team to cheer you on, I highly suggest you change the starting roster of your team. Or, better yet, clear the bench.

Lastly, and most importantly, to my husband. The pride I take in us, more than anything, makes my posture change and my heart burst from the infinite love I have for you. And for us. And how we looked each other in the eye in our darkest and hardest moment and said nothing else matters anymore, other than you and me. I love you.

August 19, 2017

I looked around at where I was. I was with my best friend, Paige, and her friend, Tonya. We were wrapping up a weekend of winery tours, staying in an unbelievable house on a walnut orchard, and finally seeing Brian Ferry and Roxy Music at the Santa Barbara Bowl. It was just magical there at dusk, and you can look out over the landscape of Santa Barbara from the venue. It was one of those trips that sometimes would make you pinch yourself that this is *your* life and this is what is happening to *you*.

At the concert, we sang every song and danced the entire night through. I teared up as they sang "Avalon," our first dance song at our wedding. At the end of the night, we hugged each other tight, and I held those memories even tighter in my heart.

It reminded me of my last epic trip to Europe with my wonderful friends, when we three women traveled through Hungary, Austria, and Slovakia to see (and eventually meet) Depeche Mode. That was, of course, another thoughtfully planned trip with, again, body-pinching moments I just never want to forget.

Sitting in Santa Barbara, I was the luckiest woman, girl, mother, and wife, to be able to experience the world and take these trips. I had been told by my husband, Dana, that I needed to take them to recharge and regroup, to have time to get back to myself. Time to spend with friends. Time to not be a mother for a while. And definitely time to not be a wife. And it was *definitely* time to get back to appreciating being a girl, woman, mother, and wife.

From California, I texted my family to be sure all of my carefully laid out plans for the kids' sports events, school necessities, alarms set for school, and all of the things I had spent the weekend trying to forget. Prior to leaving on this trip, my anxiety had been on overdrive, as the kids' calendar seemed so complicated and likely would not be followed by my husband, despite my numerous attempts to be *sure* he understood what he needed to do while I would be gone. I mean, he is a *man*! How in the world could he possibly keep track of everything I needed him to do?

I am a necessity. I am the organizer. I am so important. And I will be so missed while I am gone.

August 20, 2017

Buellton, California

I am going to be so sad to go home. This was one of my most favorite trips with my very favorite friend. We lay by a beautiful pool with a Zen garden. We sunbathed while looking over the beautiful hills and valleys. We listened to the new soundtrack of the movie, *Atomic Blonde* and danced around the grounds and the beautiful house. Goats bleated just below us as they grazed the grasses in a politically-correct, environmentally friendly, true California way.

We spoke about all of the girls' dating woes. How the men in Los Angeles were vapid, unavailable users of their hearts, their wallets, and their time. But yet, they still would never dream of leaving California.

How envious they were that I was on this trip but could still be a mom and wife when I went home, without skipping a beat. I became more than ready to head back home to Denver to the welcoming arms of my children and my loving husband.

August 21, 2017

Denver, Colorado

God, I love flying by myself. It is so easy and comfortable. I just needed to be sure my husband was picking me up from the airport, and he did.

When I landed, Dana was so cheerful and happy to see me. Huge hugs, huge kisses, and huge laughs as he drove me home. I looked at him and felt so grateful for him and his love for me.

Their weekend without me was uneventful, apparently. He said he'd had a few friends over to the house that weekend to play cards and have some drinks. Translation: the house will be a disaster, and he is dropping me off to take care of that before he heads to work.

Messes that I didn't make. Food that I'd shopped for before I left that wasn't there now, food I will have to shop for again, now that I was home. I was certain there would be laundry that needed to get done, including some laundry I had left behind in the hopes someone would notice and do it. And here we go again…

That evening's dinnertime was uneventful, as well. The kids told me all about their weekend. They sometimes get annoyed when people stay too late at the house and drink too much. They get annoyed when our mutual friends are too loud, because they can't get to sleep.

My youngest son explained that the soccer tournament his team was in while I was gone was completely torturous. His team was levelled by their opponents, and he didn't want to talk about it. I reviewed homework assignments for the following day for both boys, much to their chagrin. And let the parenting battles commence…

Finally, the boys were in bed. They were clearly exhausted from lack of sleep and the eventful weekend at our house, filled with loud adults. Finally with some time to catch up, Dana and I talked about his weekend and mine. I confided in him how grateful I was to go on this trip. We kissed on the couch. Then we made love, holding each other and promising not to have petty, meaningless fights anymore.

August 22, 2017

Crap. I was definitely exhausted now. That stupid alarm on my phone was just relentless. I ended up waking up feeling loved but exhausted from the night before. No time for the weary, however, because we were right back to the before-school morning routine.

Crap, do I have to drive carpool? I had better check to see if I am signed up on the computer sign-up, to be sure. I was sure I could probably drive the boys in my pajamas... Who really cares, anyway? I do. I care, but not that morning. I was exhausted.

Again, I needed to check this dumb carpool Sign-Up Genius form (that I created, mind you), while trying to figure out if, indeed, I was signed up to drive the middle schoolers to school. Unfortunately, I ended up having to yell up to my children to get a move on and get ready for school.

Shit. I *was* driving carpool that day, which meant I had fifteen minutes before I had to leave to pick up four more middle-school-aged rays of sunshine. After checking the carpool sign-up, I discovered it also appeared my oldest had left his Google classroom account open. It must have been for his assignment that day. I remember I *definitely* listed that on my list of things to do while I was gone. They probably didn't do it. I decided I'd better find out to be sure, because it was certainly something they'd missed, but I didn't.

The tab open on my desktop was a phone number attached to a Gmail account, not a middle-school email account. Weird, because it was not at all familiar to me. So, I read the emails that were open in the tabs. I read all of them. Every sneaky, deceitful, lying, and cheating text and email.

The messages had been going back and forth for months. They were not from my son, but between my lovely husband and another woman. And it was someone I knew, or thought I knew, very well...

I swiftly swallowed bile mixed with my morning coffee as my kids walked into the office while I was reading through those emails and text messages. Without missing a beat, I told my boys to get their shoes on, because we would be late for carpool.

I swallowed my bile again and fought back tears as though holding up the very foundation of my life. I glanced at the clock on my computer and realized I had exactly eight minutes to pick up four other kids who were not mine. There was no time to be upset, to cry, to scream, or to examine what I had just discovered.

I proceeded to slap myself in the face in the bathroom. Twice. I told myself, "Erin, snap out of this. You have to be Mom right now." I also thought about how I could not act on the feelings that began bubbling up inside me.

Erin, you have to be responsible. Again. You don't get to be YOU right now.

I sent the boys to the car outside and walked into my husband's room. We had stopped sleeping in the same bedroom together many, many years ago for our own sanity and need for sleep. I was also long past feeling embarrassed that we had already started to resemble a 1950s couple. Truthfully, that situation didn't affect our sex life at all. I mean, come on, we'd just been intimate the night before, because I had been gone on a trip. We had argued before I left, and we'd both realized we needed to make up and make things right.

Calmly, I called out to Dana and asked him to join me in the office. I opened one of the many disturbing emails and text messages and showed them to him without a second thought. Bluntly, I asked him to explain what I had just discovered and then read some of them out loud.

In only seconds, the blood drained from his face and his eyes welled up with tears. I screamed at him to not touch or delete anything on that screen and keyboard, as I'd already begun to print each and every email and message, certain that I was going to need proof.

And just like that, I got into my car and drove away to do my duty as a mom. I drove the carpool of grouchy early-morning middle-school boys to school. I do remember driving out of my driveway, but that was about it for that trip.

Everything was, and still is, different than before. So now, I thought to myself, what do we do? The better question, honestly, was what do I do?

I ended up thinking that we needed to go back to the beginning...

1990

I was walking home from my freshman year of high school. I hated walking home from school alone, as it always made me feel like a loser, a loner.

As I walked through my neighborhood by myself, feeling like a complete loser, I saw my friend walking ahead of me with a skinny, tall dude. I called out to her and ran to catch up with them. She introduced me to her friend, Dana, who was quite nice, polite, and handsome. We introduced ourselves, made each other laugh, and made plans for later.

I left to continue on to my house, and they went on their way. *Hmm*, I thought. *Well, wasn't he pretty sweet and cute?*

I went over to my friend's house later that night. Frankly, her house was notorious for debauchery—no parents, no rules, all of the alcohol and marijuana you wanted, and all of the sleepovers and sex. It was the perfect excuse to propose a sleepover to my uber-strict parents, and they agreed. When I arrived there, we all played pool and drank beer, and that cute boy and I kissed. I was totally smitten. And so was he.

Inevitably, that cute boy and I ended up together as a couple. We broke up and rekindled our relationship many times through high school. We made some good decisions together and, more than often, really bad ones, as well. I saw my life going in a different, less strict, direction, and I couldn't wait to start that life. I have countless memories of our escapades. In high school, my best girlfriends and I loved to go dancing. Every. Single. Weekend. We went when we were allowed, and we went when we weren't allowed, either. After meeting my new cute guy, I remembered he was part of the group of sexy guys who would dance to the same song every Friday night at one of our favorite dance clubs. Even before I actually met him, I just knew I needed to meet him, but I never knew how.

Eventually, that problem was solved, and I decided to go dancing every Friday with my girlfriends where he and his friends went dancing, too. I danced there every Friday, if I could. I made myself obnoxiously obvious to him. I would stare at him, incessantly.

He was bad-boy "cool" to me. And once we actually met and spent time together, we were immediately and electrically attracted to each other.

He saw me in a way no one in my life ever had before. He loved the dichotomy of a straight-and-narrow girl who, in reality, was neither. He loved the idea of a girl who had proper, financially stable parents, but also a girl who was willing to do *anything* to spend time with him. Especially when I was not supposed to.

August 22, 2017

You know that feeling when everything feels different than it did before? For me, it was immediately after I had driven both carpool duty for my older son and, afterward, drove my younger son to elementary school. I looked around at everything in my house. I skimmed over all of my beautiful things, my beautiful home, my sense of security, and none of it mattered anymore. I didn't want any of it anymore. I had that nauseating feeling of wanting to burn that life of mine to the ground. It was terrifying.

Then there were my sons. That same day, I decided never to tell them what had happened. I knew, if I planted the seed that their father was so deceitful, they would never look at him the same. And moreover, they might follow in his footsteps when they were older and do the same to their spouses... I hated my husband for that. For making me have to make the responsible choices, while he deliberately chose not to do the same. But in truth, I hated the idea of my sons having to navigate all of this and lose their innocence. So, I kept quiet.

On the day after I found out what had happened, I made an appointment to see a psychiatrist. I went into full-on triage mode, a trait I prided myself on being able to activate quite easily. I compartmentalized my life.

I walked into the office of my psychiatrist, someone who prescribed medications to me from time to time, when I needed them. All it took was one question from her about how I was doing, and we started talking and talking. I mean, I talked a lot. And I cried. I cried a lot. She couldn't believe I had just found out about my husband the day before, and already I was trying to figure out what I could do to move forward.

Truthfully, in hindsight, I think I just wanted her to give me a pill, one I could take so I could make all of this go away. I wanted her to help me disappear. Thankfully, she saw right through me and let me know this would be a long process and a pill wouldn't cut it. It felt surreal to be talking about my life, which felt like it could likely be over in just minutes.

I had to put the whole puzzle together by myself. I was grateful I had printed all the messages between the two of them, mainly because it greenlit my new career as a detective. I was able to match up the dates of their messages and remember each and every lie based on a timeline I built.

The first night after my big discovery, I kicked him out of the house. I didn't care where he went; he just couldn't be around me. We spoke on the phone briefly, but to be honest, I don't even remember what I said to him. I just remember having to keep my wits about me. Again, I didn't have the luxury of losing my head with my kids at home.

The next morning, he came back to the house, a dog with his tail between his legs. He was desperate for forgiveness and desperate for a decision from me, as if that was even a possibility after just twenty-four hours. I was desperate to not have to automatically forgive, like I always seem to do.

I told him I didn't have an answer. And I didn't know if or when I ever would. My puffy, bloodshot eyes were the glaring neon sign saying I hadn't slept. I thought that maybe I should share with him all of my vicious fantasies for how I was going to retaliate.

I kept thinking about how quickly and easily I could go backward and hurt him. I wanted to hurt him so, so much, to match my own pain. As if there was some sort of mathematical equation where I could equally transfer my pain to him, with no more substantive damage inflicted to myself. In my brain, this seemed entirely possible. And more so… feasible? But as we all know, this was the worst advice I could give myself. Still, it felt like the best advice I could give myself at the time.

I was a mother of two. And I thought of myself as a responsible parent (most of the time). I would be lying if I didn't worry about what others would think of me. My internal circle, and pretty much the outer-lying five circles of friends and family, would all eventually know our dirty secret. My thought was that that revelation just *couldn't* happen: my financial investments and my social investments would take a foundational leveling, from which I believed I would never recover.

I liked to think I was pragmatic and thinking clearly at the time. Obviously, this was just about as far from the truth as Australia is from Vancouver. Truth be told, I barely remember any of it. I drove the kids to practices, and I talked to the regular group of parents as if things were perfectly fine. I remember standing on the sidelines at my son's soccer practice, praying that someone, *anyone*, wouldn't notice that I wasn't myself, that I was definitely not okay.

In hindsight, I would like to thank the Academy for awarding me an Oscar for my performances in those early days. No one actually came with awards or medals, though. Instead, I was awarded the prize of unwavering sadness, anxiety, illness, and bad decisions. Then there was my bonus prize, as well: attempting to remain normal and happy for my kids and trying to keep my appearance unscathed.

Standing on the sidelines of another average Tuesday-night soccer practice, I noticed many of the team dads were there, but no moms. The dads were chatting, laughing, and unflinchingly congratulating one another for their accomplishments. And then there was me, who had refused to retire from my mom duties, because they were *mine*. And I was fine, right?

What a fucking self-destructive and ridiculous joke.

Next thing I remember, I was walking into a marriage counselor's office with him. I pretended to be there for more than the emotional decimation of my spouse. But I wanted revenge. I really wanted to exude the kind of anger that all of the movies say I was supposed to have.

Wasn't I supposed to throw all of his shit into a dumpster, set it on fire, and head off on a girls' trip somewhere exotic? The kind of a trip where I'd meet some amazingly hot yoga instructor who made me feel like a princess and would teach me how to make my own kombucha?

Well, that didn't happen, because I chose to stay and try to figure out the shitshow that our marriage had become. We went to that marriage counselor together, but only once. Afterward, I convinced myself that seeing her would be more damaging than just trying to get through it ourselves, so why go back over and over again? It only felt like I was ripping the Band-Aid off. So, I wrapped myself in my pride and ego, in a veiled attempt to prove how "strong" I was.

And then, my dear friend Marie, in whom I'd confided, was diagnosed with breast cancer. I sat in her kitchen while she told me something I just could not fathom being true. The weird lump she'd felt while putting away her groceries had turned out to be a malignant tumor. And somehow, the universe gave her this awful thing, which weirdly also gave me something to occupy my attention, love, and devotion.

It wasn't a positive experience, obviously. It was a terrifying experience that I couldn't even wrap my head or heart around. But for me, it was somewhat positive in that it concretized a friendship we both really needed at that time. And, selfishly, it offered a level of distraction that I needed, to avoid my own life.

Ultimately, she came out cancer-free on the other end. And I came out okay on the other side, too.

I know that leaning on friends is something women do a lot. But this type of "lean-in" was almost primal. For both of us, I think. I will say this over and over again. Women, especially my women, are my chosen family. Nothing will cement that into your own DNA more profoundly than horrible, life-altering experiences. Marie needed comedic distractions, something this extremely self-deprecating girl is tops at providing. And I needed her to be in my life and to not leave it. She didn't, and I will be forever grateful to have her in my life.

"Pain is inevitable. Suffering is optional," wrote author Haruki Murakami and probably the Dalai Lama and lots of other wise people.

I can add that suffering feels so much less painful when you surround yourself with unconditional friendships. And let's be honest, female friendships are the shit.

Being Uncomfortable

L et's talk about being uncomfortable. What does that mean for you? Self-help Instagram influencers will tell you that being uncomfortable means you should drink more mushroom tea, increase your own daily meditations and affirmations, start your day with bulletproof coffee instead of regular java, get working on your vegan diet, refuse the negative energy suckers in your life, start a 401K (if you can), swap out your gas-guzzling SUV for something electric that will never suffice for what kind of vehicle you actually need, forever be a "work in process" at not offending those around you who are so very easily offended, get a chamomile enema to cleanse your colon, refuse to listen to "ABC" by the Jackson 5 or Billie Jean, or do anything that could cause anyone else to pause for their own "triggers," use non-aluminum deodorant, be aware of your own ability to offend anyone and everyone around you at any given time, own your responsibility for things you are not even responsible for and hold onto that guilt forever, raise your sons to be forever fearful of being themselves, and never, *ever* question anything listed above.

I will go ahead and say, "*Fuck. That.*" Nope. No, thank you. That is not going to happen in my life, at least not anymore.

Frankly, I have had it with that mentality. I can safely say that the mentality I have described above is not sustainable, nor is it healthy at all. This is all in my own humble opinion and mine, alone. I never took a survey of other people. However, I know that the majority of people around me likely agree with me.

The abundant assumption that floats around in this world we live in today is that the world owes everyone something. I think subscribing to entitled beliefs of that kind is an incredible and ridiculous farce.

The mother in me, of course, wants to insulate my kids from the ills of the world, while still encouraging my sons to sharpen their teeth in the real world. And there, my friends, is one of the great parenting dilemmas.

I am forever grateful for the hardships and life lessons that I, myself, have experienced and endured. They have all led ultimately to my own well-being, as a result. Mainly, I think, because I used those experiences to season my future experiences.

What I do not understand, and maybe what I will never understand, is how people use some of their worst experiences to excuse their own worst behaviors. What gives people the right to excuse away their bad choices and questionable character traits, all under the guise of being seasoned by their previous decisions?

Maybe I am harsh, callous, uncaring, and likely someone who has witnessed some of the worst of humanity. Or maybe it is because of the horrors of my own poor decisions growing up, circumstances I unwittingly was involved in. The life lessons I never really ever wanted that ended up pressing me into a mold I never would have fit into.

What do you do with that self-realization? Do you push your children to fail and hope that they, too, push themselves into their own self-sufficient mold of an adult, like I had to? These days, I just don't believe that it is an option anymore. But there *is* the option of honesty: with yourself and maybe with your own children. I revel in honesty about things I never anticipated sharing with anyone else. The kind of honesty I definitely never wanted to share with even my own children, and only shared when they were able to fully absorb it, of course.

I have had some uncomfortable conversations with my kids. This writing project has forced the honesty trump card to be played again, again, and again. I had tried to keep the subject matter of this book under wraps until I was fully able to explain it to them in the best possible way. There *had* to be a perfect situation in which to talk about all of this, right?

No. There wasn't and there never would be a perfect situation and time to finally talk to my kids about all of the contents of this book. For our little family, the conversation happened innocently and organically around a Thanksgiving table together.

Each year, I force my sons and husband, sometimes begrudgingly, to voice out loud their gratitude devotions from the previous year and for the upcoming year, as well. They placate me and participate with ample eye-rolling, of course. When my kids were young, their devotions were pretty simplistic and innocent. They were grateful for their

Xbox, their iPhones, their dogs, their friends, etc. As they have grown, their gratitudes have become far more reflective and introspective.

So, this last one was not any different. My oldest son gave thanks for his friends and his new girlfriend and his health. My husband explained how grateful he was to have a simpler work environment, thankful for his family and marriage, and thankful for his health, as well. Then my youngest child said he was grateful that his parents were still married, not divorced, and have not had any majorly big problems that would cause his own life to be disrupted or harder than he already felt it was.

For some strange reason, both my husband and I looked at each other and realized that this may very well be the most perfect lead-in to explain our previous marital problems to our kids. We had, until that night, tried to come up with the best possible scenario for when and how to describe our past problems, his past indiscretions, and our hard-earned new path as the Hunts 2.0. With only a glance, we both understood that there was no time like the present to just explain everything to our sons as best as we could.

My husband looked at both boys, took a deep breath, and said, "Well, your dad isn't perfect. At all. I made a huge mistake and hurt your mom a few years ago, but we have worked our asses off to get through it and keep our family together." Or something to that effect.

I think I blacked out as he finally explained to our boys how our lives had changed so drastically, several years ago. He fell on his own proverbial sword and owned his terrible decisions, while explaining how our marriage and family were our first and most important responsibility.

My youngest son looked at me with an uneasy laugh, expecting me or my husband to drop our punchline on what *surely* must be a joke. But neither of us did. In fact, I said very little to either of the boys and let my husband navigate how this conversation would go around this very uncomfortable subject.

He explained how he still, to that day, wasn't exactly sure why he did what he did. And he explained that he was so grateful our family was still intact, that their mother had been willing to stay and help to make that happen, and how he and I had done a *tremendous* amount of work in order to make all of those things true.

The room remained silent for a while. Then, as they thought of them, they asked us both questions. Instead of trying to rescue the situation and the conversation, I decided to pass that baton of responsibility to my husband.

And he actually ran with it, in a way I can only describe as something I am so very proud of. We decided to turn what could have been such an awful and difficult situation into what I had always hoped this particular conversation would look and sound like.

I hope my kids will remember that moment with grace and truly understand that their parents are real human beings, full of flaws and mistakes. But their parents were also not willing to walk away from their family. Rather, they chose to walk toward it and work hard to keep it. And yes, it was a gut-wrenchingly uncomfortable conversation that I wasn't prepared to have.

In my mind, I had my own PowerPoint presentation detailing my exercises for trying to keep our family (and my shit, for that matter) together. This life often has a different plan for us, though, doesn't it? And while my husband and I ripped off the Band-Aid and had the dreaded conversation with our kids about our marital woes, I realized how our little family had a crazy ability to, again, roll with the punches. Don't we all, especially when you have no other choice?

While that conversation was incredibly uncomfortable, it was also such a gift. The conversations we four have had since then have been utterly enlightening. Almost something I wish I would have had when I was my children's age with my own parents. And while I know there is a fine line between oversharing and not sharing enough with our kids, this whole writing project has really forced that issue to the forefront. It has forced me to jump into the uncomfortable head-first.

I eventually began to reframe this feeling to include how to overcome the uneasiness of being uncomfortable. I read somewhere that if you try to keep everything comfortable, what you are really doing is keeping everything the same, keeping it simple, and not thrusting your life into everything that it could be. If you were to ask someone what they wanted out of their life, do you think they would they say they want it to stay simple? I really don't think so. I think they would say they want *everything* out of their life. The simple stuff *and* the not-so simple stuff, too. I have tried to use this lens more often in looking at my life. Sometimes, the difficult stuff is only difficult when you view it *as* difficult.

There is another thing I have tried to incorporate more often, too. When I was a kid, it felt like all I ever heard from adults was, "No." No to my requests, no to my wishes, no to off-the-wall situations. Just *no*. All the time.

And on top of that, I was punished for all of it. Often. Of course, this was just my perspective. I am certain it wasn't really as bad as it seemed in my head at the time. Nonetheless, the residual memories of that negativity left an indelible imprint on me.

I do not want my kids to feel that way when they look back on their own childhoods. So, I try to say *yes* more often than I say *no* to them, within reason. When my initial snap response to their request is, "Absolutely not," I try to pause and consider why I am saying no to begin with. Is it because I am uncomfortable? Is it because it is easier to just say no? Is it because I am uneasy saying yes? Likely all of the above.

I revel in the uncomfortable now. I kind of love living in that space I used to avoid like the plague. The space between my anxiety telling me not to say or do anything to cause waves and my doing the exact opposite, to see if it as bad as I've imagined in my own head. And, spoiler alert, it is more often than not a *fallacy*. It actually is the opposite of unsettling, and it gives me an empowering feeling of welcoming the uncomfortable.

From time to time, when that pit in my stomach becomes undeniable, I have to remind myself to sit and marinate in that feeling, before I push it away.

England

England. Back in the nineties, the music of England, the style of England, the fashion of England—all of it was intoxicating to me. I was a sophomore in high school at the time, and I began to think I didn't belong at home in Colorado anymore. I believed I belonged somewhere bigger, better, and more exciting. I just didn't know how or where to go.

But let's press rewind for a second.

A year prior, when I was a freshman, my social life had begun to spiral out of control. While my parents were distracted with my brother and his own troubles with school, I deliberately flew under their radar. This, in turn, would greenlight anything and everything I wanted to do, whenever and wherever I could.

I wouldn't go to school when I was supposed to and constantly lied to my parents about it. Back then, ditching school could be excused by a simple note from a parent. And while my mother's signature was unbelievably strange, my father's signature was easily forgeable.

I smoked cigarettes incessantly; I drank alcohol any chance I could get. I would ditch school and go get high. I jumped out of my window at night to sneak away with friends. I stole my family's car and drove around after they went to sleep. I partied more and more with my friends, and my deceptions and lies to my parents became almost unbearable to continue. When I did eventually get caught by my parents, the punishment was the same each and every time. I was grounded, over and over again. It happened so often, it became a running joke with my friends. At one point, I counted the number of days I had been grounded but lost count after passing the two-month mark. While it was exhilarating at the time, in hindsight, it was exhausting.

Ultimately, my behavior and problems came to a head with my parents. I realized, as did my parents, that staying at my current high school would not end well. Frankly, my older brother had attended the same school before me and then transferred to another high school due to somewhat similar circumstances. So, for some reason, my parents and I were able to discuss options we could both agree on without my having to be grounded yet again. It was astounding!

My best friend, Paige, (who was actually in equal trouble but far better at getting away with things than I was) and I both decided we needed a change. We decided, if we were going to leave our high school, it would be far easier if we did it together. Our parents collectively agreed.

She and I decided to hedge our bets on a school we could both agree on and applied to one of the two all-girls Catholic schools in Denver. In order to attend that school, you were required to take an entrance exam at the school, in their library. The best way to describe the computer station at this library was as a *Pretty in Pink* moment, when

Andrew McCarthy and Molly Ringwald exchanged completely ridiculous quips on ancient computers.

Paige and I gazed at each other with sarcastic giggles and smiles as the test-taking began. But that ended quickly, when we discovered the other test-taking girls were far from fond of Paige and me. And they made their feelings known.

This little suburban girl and her suburban best friend realized that the disgust emanating from the other students around us could (and likely would, in the near future) result in a fight. More specifically, it would result in a fight with *many* girls. It was terrifying to us both. We had presented this plan to both of our parents, and at that moment, we both knew we were making a colossal mistake.

I went back to my parents and explained the situation, asking if I could look at another option for myself. Somehow, I convinced them, truly by the skin of my teeth, to agree to a different option for me. They were willing to let me try something else. Which I did. There was a brand-new high school opening in my local school district, and they were accepting students. It felt like a life raft, and I wanted to grab that raft and paddle away. I just had a feeling in my heart and soul that my life would rapidly become a dumpster fire, if I stayed at that first high school, so I left and I began to attend a brand-new high school the following year.

It was my chance at a fresh start. It began to feel like a brand-new me and fresh opportunities were there to grab.

When this new high school opened, it swiftly became a scandalous thing. First, because the monstrously huge school was built on an old, radioactive landfill. The community, the families, the students, and the faculty had been assured the environment was safe. They had delayed the opening of the school to ensure that they had undertaken every safety precaution, evaluation, and assurance necessary. I have always thought how funny it was that things had become so bad with me, my parents actually sent me to what was called "Toxic High," instead of leaving me where I was.

It was perfect. I was a sophomore, but our sophomore class ended up as the oldest class in the school that year, in order to build the student body population. So, really, I felt like I was a senior in high school every year. I had wonderful friends, met even more wonderful ones, and our class made our mark each and every year thereafter, by developing and exploring new school traditions.

During that first year I was there, my school also welcomed exchange students, but I cannot remember exactly where they came from. I *do* remember, however, how exotic it seemed that they had travelled to a completely different country all on their own (albeit living with a host family), but I nonetheless thought it was super-cool.

When junior year began, and while our school was still basically a toddler, my friend Talia and I asked about the exchange program. The school was busy building its brand and attempting to avoid any more scandals, despite some widely publicized staff infidelities, which seemed to be a thing at our school. Between the scandal of being "Toxic High" and various affairs among staff members in the school, reporters parked in front of the building, hoping for news and interviews. Students and staff were instructed not to speak to them. They even illegally wandered our school hallways in search of an exclusive interview or new details on the scandalous things going on at "Toxic High."

So, regarding the exchange student program at my school, it occurred to me that an "exchange" is usually two-sided. If someone comes here, then who is going to the other country?

I like to chalk up this next development to luck and timing. My friend and I talked to our school about the possibility of sending the two of us somewhere, to make the exchange a reality. We did assume the administration would immediately dismiss our request. I certainly never imagined the opposite. But that is what happened!

Once we had the school on board, next up were our families. Again, putting my assumptions to shame, my parents and hers also got right on board. So, we began to plan our adventure overseas. Although I had been studying French for some time, I wasn't confident enough to move to another non-English-speaking country.

We ended up in England. The south of England, to be precise. A little village between Devon and Cornwall called Ivybridge. My friend ended up in a host family's home close to our school, or *college* as high school is called there. I, however, was matched with a family who lived in a quaint, lovely cottage much farther away, on the ocean.

While it was breathtaking, perhaps a major contender for the next Nancy Meyers movie, it was also isolated. The family had a daughter my age who was brutally shy and quiet. She never offered to spend time with me or go anywhere, and oftentimes just holed up in her room, leaving me to fend for myself. My parents called once a week to check in with me. As this was my idea, I was not honest with them about my loneliness. I just told them it was fun and beautiful and that Talia and I were doing fine. But I was way too far from Talia, geographically, to see her regularly; really, only when we attended school. This wasn't exactly what either of us had hoped for or planned.

So, I wasn't actually fine. I was lonely and depressed and wanted to go home. But I also did not want to accept defeat. Make no mistake, this family was lovely and kind. They brought a complete stranger into their home and did their best to make me feel welcome. They helped me if I needed something and provided me with my own room and transportation to and from school.

I don't remember exactly how old their cottage was, but it was old. The ceilings were incredibly low, the plaster on the walls was ancient and placed there by hand, and normally refrigerated items were kept in their pantry, or "cupboard," to save space. It felt confining and suffocating to me, especially because of my distance from basically anyone. My escape was visiting the ocean, which was in their backyard. I appreciated the greenery, rolling hills, and real beauty of that place.

The other members of my host family were nice enough but odd, which makes where and how they lived much easier to understand. I tried to make it work with that family. I really did. And given how I was raised, I knew I shouldn't ruffle feathers, shouldn't complain, that I could make myself happy and force my smile—even if I was lonely and unhappy.

But something deep down told me this was not sustainable. That staying in their home long-term was not feasible, and I needed to change the situation myself.

The teacher who had helped coordinate the exchange with our high school back home was our advocate, counselor, and contact, while we were there in Ivybridge. One day, I spoke candidly with him about my experiences thus far. How unbelievably shitty I felt even complaining, but how my loneliness was stifling and I didn't want to offend this family by saying so. They were stiff-upper-lip Brits, and I didn't know how they would or could help me, but I was certain they would be offended by this dumb American.

I believe my counselor felt guilty and responsible for my unhappiness, mainly as he had paired me with this family. It was clear, while he may be a great teacher, unfortunately, he was a terrible matchmaker. So, he decided to open his home to me, as an alternative placement. He had a wife and two small boys, and they lived far closer to my friend, as well as to our school. In essence, it was a godsend, and I, again, felt incredibly lucky to have a second chance. I didn't give up and go home. I took a different path and tried again with a new family.

School there was quite different and yet the same. It was hard, harder than our school in Colorado, but not impossible. Slowly, Talia and I made friends at school. We were befriended by teachers there and came out of our shells as we acclimated to all of it.

Prior to leaving the U.S., the seeds of independence had been planted in me. I wanted it so badly. But it was in England where I really learned how to be independent. Well, as independent as I could be. My parents wired money to me each week, and I would walk to the bank in our small village to make withdrawals. I had a paper balance book for my account and learned how to convert dollars to pounds. I learned how to navigate the little town, and eventually my friend and I began to venture out beyond the village a bit.

I learned that, after school, students from my school would join our teachers at the small pub in the village to talk about the school day over pints. It was a completely different world, and I loved it. That feeling of growing up and of independence continued to blossom. I would be lying if I said the pub lifestyle wasn't provocative and interesting for a young American girl. But, as it is often said, drinking there was understood, handled responsibly, and, bottom line—not a big deal.

Our school had an art history trip planned for the Tuscany region of Italy. My friend and I were actually able to go along with them. As a teenager, this was most certainly another pinch-me moment, one I'd never really expected back when we'd originally proposed going on this exchange. But man, I'll be forever grateful that we could make it happen.

We left from the white cliffs of Dover with a group from the school, taking the ferry across the English Channel. Talia and I stood at the back of the ferry, with the wind blowing and the waters choppy beneath us, and we both giggled in disbelief. Mind you, back inside the ferry, our classmates were green-faced, trying not to puke on one other, or they were running out the doors to throw-up overboard.

The ferry docked in Calais, France, and we took a train through France and Switzerland, into the north of Italy, arriving in Florence. We spent a week there with our classmates and teachers, going to museums, cathedrals, and restaurants, while staying in a hostel that was full of us British and American students. We visited Pisa (yes, the tower was still leaning), Siena, and Luca. Each stop was breathtaking and beautiful; there were picture-taking opportunities everywhere. At the end, we returned to England the same way we'd arrived, via the vomit-inducing ferry across the English Channel. I don't know if it because of our time away or some of our other experiences there, but again, a switch flipped for me. I felt alive, independent, myself, and it was liberating.

When we returned, my friend and I decided to venture to Portsmouth to see a band that had become extremely popular in England. The concert was ridiculously fun. We sang every song, danced, and made memories. When the concert was over, we both looked at each other, crestfallen, wishing it hadn't ended. As we walked out of the venue, we passed a catering van that had its doors open, while caterers in black aprons were scurrying to bring trays of food somewhere. Who needs catering like that after a concert? Two words. The. Band.

We looked at each other slyly, grabbed some trays of food and a couple of aprons, and became two of the newest employees of said catering company. We followed the rest of the legitimate employees into a room filled with music, laughing, drinking, smoke, and the band.

After placing the food down, we removed our aprons and casually sat down, making every effort to appear like we belonged there. Before we knew it, we did! We drank, laughed, and talked with the band and their management. Eventually, with liquid courage, we spilled the beans about what had preceded our meeting them. Thankfully, this was met with an equal amount of laughter, along with their utmost respect for our ingenuity. We ended up going to their follow-up show at another venue shortly thereafter. Although we weren't able to pull off our catering escapade there, it made for yet another memory I will never forget. I remain to this day eternally grateful to have had that experience with Talia.

As my time in England began to come to an end, my time with my host family became more and more difficult. When I first moved in with my host family, my teacher and his wife were warm, welcoming, and lovely to live with. They helped with my transition, talked to me about my experiences and feelings, and I grew close with their children. Kind of like an older sister to their sons. But as time progressed, tensions began to grow. I didn't understand it.

As a teenage girl, I didn't understand what I had done wrong. I always helped out around their house and helped with their kids whenever I could. I cleaned my room and cooked for the family. I never asked for more than I should have from them and felt like my footprint in their lives was as gentle as it could be. I checked in often with my teacher, to show my appreciation for his taking me in and helping make this experience so great for me, despite its beginning. The parents cooked meals for me, too, ones I liked and sometimes requested. They tried to introduce me to more traditional English food, some of which I did not like, but I pretended I did out of courtesy. Like a good girl and guest, I always said thank you.

Although it seemed odd and frivolous to them, I bathed every day. That is how the conflict began. First were the snide comments about my American need to shower frequently. How dare I? Then, the teacher's wife made me kidney pie for dinner one night, and I just couldn't do it. It smelled like an autopsy in their kitchen, and I just couldn't stomach the idea of eating it.

I did try, of course, because that's what you do to appease others, instead of being honest with yourself. I ate two bites while the entire family stared at me from their kitchen table. The first bite was shocking, but I swallowed it. I lied and said, "*Mmm*. Yum."

By the second bite, I threw up into my mouth and then proceeded to swallow that second bite of kidney pie with a side of vomit. I couldn't tell the difference between the two. When asked, I, of course, said graciously, "Thank you for making the effort to make this for me. You are so kind and thoughtful!"

The mother's next statement was something to the effect of, if I enjoyed it that much, she would make it for me all the time. I bluntly blurted out that I was lying and to *never* make it for me again. It was like I had vomited those words as well.

Her face fell, and the rage brewed up inside her. I saw the change and felt embarrassed, realizing her feelings were hurt. I fervently apologized, but it didn't matter. I tried every reason to explain to her why I wasn't prepared for that meal or to eat that kind of food, mainly blaming my American constitution for my inability to handle the organ meat flavors and smells. But, it didn't appease her.

I tucked my tail between my legs, then washed every dish and cleaned the kitchen before going to bed feeling like the worst houseguest on the planet. Again, though—kidney fucking pie? What was she thinking?

A few days later, I learned exactly what she was thinking. Their kids had been put to bed, and I was in bed as well. But I had homework to finish and wanted to make tea before I went to sleep, so I crept into their kitchen, trying not to disturb anyone, and filled the kettle.

My teacher and his wife were in their backyard. Their voices had always been gentle, kind, sweet. But they weren't gentle then. My teacher's wife was upset and angry. I assumed they were arguing about him, about not cleaning the house or putting the "rubbish" out. But it was about *me*. She berated him with accusations that he was attracted to me. That I was flirting with him in their home. That, if that were the case, what could he and I be up to while at school, away from her watchful eyes?

I was mortified and terrified. I was seventeen years old and he was forty-four. I was thousands of miles away from home. He was one of the kindest teachers I had ever met. But I knew right then and there it was time for me to go home. This was far too much for me to handle. All by myself.

So, I wrapped things up with school and ended up leaving Talia and heading back to the U.S. She stayed longer and was upset with my quick exit from the UK. She stayed as long as I was supposed to have stayed. I had left under the guise of being devastatingly homesick, saying I needed to come home and that was that.

I felt such tremendous guilt in telling Talia that I was leaving earlier than expected, but staying with my host family was untenable. Impossible. And I didn't want to cause any more problems for my teacher, his family, and his marriage.

The foreshadowing isn't lost on me. But you do not know what you don't know. He was such a generous host for me, for which I am forever grateful. But after I left, I never heard from him or his family again. As a grown woman now, I understand exactly why. But I wouldn't change a thing about any of it. I know people speak of formative experiences. This is one of my top ten.

As I mentioned before, this sparked a fierce independence in me. I came back home after living on my own, more or less. Rules and limits had become foreign concepts to me. I remember asking my parents, "What does independence mean to *you*? Do either of you remember the first time you opened your own wings to fly?"

My wings were ready to fly as soon as I returned to the USA.

The Hustle

After I returned from England, when I was still only seventeen years old, Dana and I decided we would move out together and start living on our own. We decided to rent a small house in downtown Denver. It was in an area called Uptown, which definitely wasn't a good part of town. Looking back, it was total insanity that any landlord would allow two kids sign a lease at all. But we definitely put on a good "mature for their age"show, so the two owners of the little house signed off on our lease. We were off to the races of being grown-ups.

Why, oh why, did we want to be grown-ups so fast? We had sealed our fate in becoming independent, learning life's pitfalls along the way.

Our house was behind the back entrance to a coffee shop. In our world, it was *the* coffee shop. My husband's long-time friend Matt's family had purchased this shop; Matt, Matt's older brother, and basically anyone else we knew who needed a job worked there, too. It was our little haven for our group of misfit friends, who, as luck would have it, were also fiercely independent, as well. Dana worked there, too, from time to time.

We hung out there every free moment we had. We would have card games, pool games, and parties in the shop after hours until the sun came up. Despite the dangerous surroundings (which I oftentimes chose to deny or ignore to the chagrin of my ever-worrying parents), it was like our little commune of like-minded friends who felt like family.

Our little house was tiny, green, and one story. It had two bedrooms, one bathroom, and a dirt-covered kitchen floor that was likely from the 1920s. At night, after 2 a.m., the dance club and bar across the street from the coffee shop offered quite a show through our bedroom windows that backed onto the alley. We often woke up in the middle of the night to hear people vomiting outside of our window after too many kamikazes and tequila shots at the club.

One night, while Dana was working at the coffee shop, the regular beat cop who patrolled the area and often checked in with us regulars at the coffee shop was working his side hustle as security at the night club. Although we knew this particular officer (he and his partner were also the owners of the house we were renting), was terrifyingly stoic and strong. He didn't tolerate *any* kind of bullshit, ever.

Dana looked across the street later that night, after hearing yelling and glass breaking, and noticed that this officer was being attacked and jumped by a number of drunken men. The officer was alone, while there were five or six drunkards having their way, beating the living shit out of him.

Without any hesitation, Dana ran across the street and struck the man pounding this cop in the head, in order to get him off of him and give our officer friend and landlord a fighting chance. And fight he did.

After Dana had reacted, punching this unlucky shithead, our cop friend got his bearings, pulled out his baton, and proceeded to show the five or six drunks that they had severely underestimated him. They all eventually either left in the back of a police cruiser or an ambulance. When all was said and done, the officer walked over to the coffee shop, cool as a cucumber, and thanked Dana for his assistance. After that, we never worried again about our neighborhood or the questionable folks we would sometimes run into. And there were many.

One hot evening in the middle of the summer, I had left the window open beside our house's front door. My lovingly sweet, well-mannered, but enormous Rottweiler, Max, was lounging on the couch in our living room. Max was my co-pilot, my shadow, and still to this day my favorite dog ever. She made living in that neighborhood wonderful. I walked with her everywhere, and only people who knew her gentile demeanor weren't afraid of her.

That night, I was cooking in our tiny little kitchen on our tiny little range. I had brought my plate to the living room to watch TV with my sweet Max when I heard a voice in the room. A disheveled drunken man who was likely high had walked up past our front yard, stuck his head into my home through the open window, and begun yelling at me to give him my food, demanding that I get him some water.

It took only a few seconds for the situation to resonate and become quite real to me. I realized quickly that a simple *no* would not suffice for this man. Without prompting by her momma, Max slowly turned her head toward and walked to the window, pacing toward it like a jaguar, emitting the lowest growl, while baring her front teeth.

This unlucky guy noticed my protective furry daughter and slowly withdrew from the window to leave. Max never needed to attack, but her presence was undoubtedly felt, terrifying him.

After he left the window, I checked the front door to make sure it was locked and saw him standing, frozen, near the sidewalk in front of my house. It seemed quite odd. I opened the door to tell him just to leave, and I wouldn't call the police. But I saw him staring at the front door of my next-door neighbor.

My neighbor was standing on his porch, a cocked shotgun in hand, and calmly told the man he should really leave before things became worse for him. And he did. That night, I became forever grateful and indebted to my neighbor.

Not long afterward, after a long shift at the coffee shop, Dana and I were sitting on our front porch, cooling off from the late-summer heat. We'd caught up on his evening and my day at work, and planned on a night of card playing with our friends later.

Halfway through our discussion, we began to hear a commotion coming toward us. We had become accustomed to the raucous nature of our neighborhood, so we assumed it was nothing and didn't give it another thought. A few minutes later, though, the screams became far louder, and closer than before.

Before we could say anything to each other, a naked woman ran screaming down the street in front of our house. We were frozen, looking at each other to confirm what we had just seen. And within seconds, a screaming naked man ran down our street after her. He was waving around a weapon in his hand, but I'm not exactly sure what it was. We didn't intervene, but we called the police, instead. In hindsight, it was another situation where the both of us remained calm and level-headed, even laughing at how bizarre living there was.

I was always hesitant to invite my parents to visit me there. I wanted to avoid their inevitable judgment around my choices, and I still wanted to break free of their hold on me. Now, as a mom of a teenager who is the same age as I was then, I cannot fathom how hard it must have been for them both to watch me break away from their home and to live in such a dangerous environment. For me though, the lessons of resilience and self-sufficiency I learned in these first stabs at independence have been lifelong gifts.

There are many T-shirts, memes, and songs filled with sayings about "the hustle." I now know that I have always surrounded myself with people who live and breathe that hustle. Those who will do whatever it takes to support themselves and their loved ones and to earn their livings in order to have the lives they want.

It may not always be glamorous. It may not always be easy. But it is always worth it.

Temptation

Temptation. While I know this topic sparks various ideas about provocative situations, places, and experiences that make us have tingly feelings of uneasiness, temptation for me is front and center in my musical and historical library. I want to fully embrace the good and the bad temptations in my life. And, cue the band, I want to start with my wonderfully decadent and good temptations: music.

Like everyone, I suppose, I have a favorite band. New Order has been my favorite band since I was in middle school. My brother and his then girlfriend lugged me along to Red Rocks as their third wheel, an annoying little sister they *never* wanted with them, and I fell deeply in love with New Order that day.

I spent every second of the concert just absorbing their music, their message, and their vibe into my mitochondria, which, to this day, has never, ever left. I danced to their music at our favorite teen dance clubs throughout the nineties. I bought every VHS video of concert footage and every compilation of their music videos (back when people actually were interested in and invested money to develop an artistic video expression of their music). I watched each and every movie that featured their music. I put stickers from each of their artistic album covers on everything I owned—my car, my camera case, my Trapper Keepers, my *anything*, to show my indelible love of their band.

And of my favorite song, "Temptation." It is a crown jewel of analogies, that I cannot deny. You can land on the inevitably obvious example of sexual temptations and indiscretions that force you to you "find your soul" on another day. Or you can read in further, to your temptations for making poor decisions with alcohol, drugs, sex, or whatever else (fill in the blank).

Temptation has always carried this dark, bleak undertone of something dire headed in my direction, a fast-moving train that is too far gone to change its trajectory. In my mind and heart, temptation was so foreboding because there was no stopping the inevitable damage it would cause, leaving me, as always, to fix things and pick up the pieces.

Isn't that what had happened in my life? And in most women's lives, since the beginning of time? My grandmothers on both sides of my family were geniuses at brokering stability for the rest of their families, often at the expense of their own happiness. Why should I be any different?

The way I was raised, suffering was not an option for women, but rather a rite of passage. For mothers, in particular. It seemed to me, based on what I was shown by my family around me, women are often not afforded the right to dwell on their feelings, to disagree, or to want more for themselves.

Make no mistake: this is not a "woke woman" statement, one where we are looking for someone to blame, using our feelings of disappointment as the litmus test. This is not, and *never* will be, part of my vernacular. I do not subscribe to this. And, I know, I will likely lose some readers here, given my insensitivity to pronouns; I don't share the public-shaming proclivity of those who may not subscribe to someone else's need to be "themselves." I just cannot do it.

I have sat in the room with *many* people who have carried on intense struggles with their own identity—to the point where that identity caused massive emotional and outright physical trauma. But if placing your preferred pronoun on your name tag at Staples, Whole Foods, or Wells Fargo, while at work, is cause for pause and making you "unable" to work? I will have to go ahead and say *no, thank you*.

I've lived through eras of horrible harassment that inevitably forced me to find my own voice. I have been raped. Repeatedly. I think I have also been a sexual aggressor, as well, at times. (Oh dear, clutch your pearls!) Because, I know, I know... How *dare* a woman admit to this? I would be an even bigger sexual hypocrite if I *didn't* speak this truth. I baited men into having sex with me, in order to make *me* feel like I had stockpiled a power supply in my personal battle bunker from my relationships. I am hard-pressed to believe that I fly solo in this regard. But I will leave ownership/membership of that to any other women willing to admit it.

So here I am, circling back to the title of my favorite song of all time, "Temptation." What does that word mean to *you*? With no judgment from me, truly be honest and ask yourself that question.

For me, with "feet to the fire" honesty, temptation means admitting the things you very rarely even admit to yourself. What you may not even admit to a best friend or anyone else you trust. Temptation, in my mind, means you have to readily accept that you (spoiler alert) are *not* without faults and you are *not* someone who makes zero mistakes. Most important, you *are* most definitely a reflection of humanity.

The hardest part, I feel, in accepting temptation is that, if you embrace the humanity of temptation in all of us weird humans, you also have to embrace that humanity in those others you may not necessarily like. Meaning, just because someone makes a mistake, even if it feels like the biggest thing ever at the time, it just might offer you the best opportunity to take a good, hard, and honest look at yourself and determine where *you* want to land.

Religion

Let's talk about religion. I was raised Catholic. Not just Catholic, but by an Irish Catholic mom. And a Catholic father. I was subjected to CCD classes, church every Sunday, nauseating Easter masses with burning frankincense that turned my stomach into a pretzel and made me feel green with nausea. All the while, I wondered why the hell people subjected themselves to these rituals. I, of course, never actually mentioned that to my family. But they could clearly tell the disdain expressed by my demeanor each and every Sunday morning. And they certainly knew how I was feeling given my teenage ambivalence toward anything I didn't want to do.

The premise and belief always were that by surrounding yourself with like-minded people, people who were certain they were all on a righteous path, these practices would inevitably put you in the fast lane to heaven. Like a "fast-pass" of self-righteousness to the Promised Land. But this whole idea always really confused me.

In our immediate and extended family, it was assumed we all would follow the path of Catholicism. There wasn't even a thought of there being another way. Our family had an unshakeable belief in all of these covenants and principles, and most importantly in the unshakeable faith-based judgments about others. Always it was presented under the guise of love, understanding, and inclusion in God's eyes.

For some reason, it *never* sat right with me. And to this day, both of my parents are devoted to higher powers. My mother's faith is more traditional, based on her upbringing as an Irish Catholic, being raised by Irish extended family in Irish Chicago. Any idea of not following every Catholic principle, tradition, and holiday was not even on the proverbial radar with her family.

Fast forward to when my parents eventually divorced. After thirty-plus years of marriage—*divorce*. This doesn't and isn't supposed to happen to true Catholics like my sweet mom. Please know, I preface this subject with a profound respect, love, and admiration for my mom. And I will get to the why of that decision later. But yes, they did divorce.

This was not due just to my father's addiction or financial naivete and irresponsibility; it was also because they just, plain grew to hate each other. My brother was not privy to a lot of the "fun" of their marriage's rapid demise, as he lived out of state and was on his own trajectory in life by that point. I had remained behind in Colorado and watched as the first bricks in their thirty-plus-year marriage began to crumble until their divorce seemed unavoidable. I will cover those lovely details later.

Mind you, my parents did love each other. They were even smitten from time to time, which always made me giggle uncomfortably, when I saw those interactions in person. But I was there and present when the end happened. I do know they loved each other, which I had seen first-hand. They had an amazing life together; they travelled and had relocated to new homes and states. My dad, the primary breadwinner, was financially sound and happy. We lived in big houses and enjoyed all of the perks those homes and what those different states afforded. If you were to whittle things down to the basic aspects of a family, my parents had me and my brother and a wonderful life with fun, friends, and love.

So, despite what has been said since by different family acquaintances, the truth is they really did love each other for a very, very long time. Eventually, however, things soured between them. I know it happened long before I caught a whiff of the resentment that they had for each other. But in the end, I was the lucky referee between them both. I had to step in with each of them, at times, when they were obviously annoyed and frustrated with the other and were saying and doing hurtful, mean-spirited things.

When my mom tearfully confided in me about her desire to leave my dad, looking for my approval, I gave it without hesitation. In my eyes, it would bring me some peace. I knew it would be rough in the beginning, but I was an adult with a family of my own. I figured I'd weathered worse things in my own life, so how bad could it be?

Things rapidly fell apart. They sold their home, split up their belongings, and seemingly shed their financial burdens. I later learned this financial split was not at all equitable, which really only fueled years and years of more problems and resentment.

I was so fucking wrong in my first reaction, and have been ever since, regarding their divorce. A definitive line in the sand was drawn, and I had to choose sides. I was never really confronted about making a decision by either parent as to whom I supported more, but the insinuation was always there. Which one did I believe more? Who did I think was more at fault? I refused to figure it out until recently. I was a perpetual fence-rider.

To the maternal side of my family, my dad was an unrepentant pariah. To the paternal side, he was a recovering alcoholic, very spiritual, loving, creative, and funny. My brother's relationship with my father is pretty limited and superficial. They speak on rare occasions, and likely that relationship will remain as such. But that is my brother's story to tell. And I will get to that later.

I mention this all under the umbrella of religion for a reason. My sweet mom, my sweet almost-nun of a mother, spent years trying to have her marriage annulled in the Catholic Church. Her quest would prove elusive but seemed absolutely necessary for her to attempt, for her own well-being in the afterlife. More times than I care to remember, she's said to me that she has needed to make clear to the Church that my dad wasn't who she thought he was or what he presented himself to be. Therefore, their marriage wasn't truthful, either.

I never agreed or even understood her thinking on this subject. Later in life, I learned it had to do with where she would land in the afterlife, which was what motivated her near obsession with an annulment—and after thirty-plus years of marriage, two kids, and a lifetime of love and memories, all of which I recall personally! It never did and still doesn't make any sense to me.

To me, religion has always felt punitive and delusional. This example just reinforced my position on the subject, even if it isn't one I really share openly or often. As you can imagine, it does not land well around my family.

Despite my stubbornness, it was anticipated and expected that I would follow the path and sacraments, including confirmation, confirming (or rather, *conforming*) that Catholicism was my religious foundation, where I would place my stake in the ground. But I never followed that path. I never believed and never agreed with the tenets, which always seemed hypocritical to me and out of alignment with my life. I never felt like I could reconcile my beliefs and lived experiences with what was expected of me in the Catholic religion.

I did try. I really, really did. I tried to complete every covenant through confirmation, because I knew how important it was to my family and extended family. But I just couldn't. By the time it was my turn to become a confirmed Catholic, I had already had an abortion, had cross-dressing and gay friends, whole-heartedly believed in birth control, and had seen the interpersonal destruction the Church could wreak. Those were the things that spoke to me; the Church consistently made me doubt myself. I felt my participation in the Catholic Church would lead me to become less than the person I knew I was. So, yet again, I dug in my heels and refused to be confirmed.

Confirmation felt to me like an utter lie to me and my family, one I just couldn't stomach for all eternity. Now I understand that I already looked to "eternity" as an explanation *and* a cause for both the good and the bad in life. I didn't need to be a Catholic to know that.

At that point in my life, my lifestyle and choices had been questionable, at best. So, presenting myself to others who fully subscribed to Catholicism as someone who also had fully adopted and surrendered to Catholic beliefs was not be possible for me. It just didn't work for me.

I would have been lying if I'd said at that time that I didn't feel disdain toward "all-in" Catholics who disliked and disapproved of those among us who made questionable decisions. That judging behavior never rang true for me. We are all faulty, fallible, and imperfect. And despite what I believed the Scriptures and Catholic tenets preached, my own questionable choices and deliberate decisions had molded me into someone the Church could never, ever welcome. And I was A-OK with that.

What does *that* say about me?

My steadfast refusal of the sacrament of confirmation has never given me pause. I knew it was the right decision for me, with no equivocation.

Yet, there were three occasions when I did have to think about or explain it again. The first was at my wedding, when my sweet Grandma Anne asked if I would reconsider getting confirmed. I swiftly shut her down and later learned my decision was devastating to her. I always chalked that up to her intense religious beliefs and upbringing. People in my family have said I should have just gone ahead with it, just acquiesced and gotten confirmed in the Catholic church for my grandmother's and mother's benefit. But I had always refused that argument. Forcing a religious tenet on me in order to appease someone else, without my wanting to do it or believing in it at all... Isn't that just a lie? Which, in my mind and heart, also isn't a great thing for a Catholic to do.

The second instance was upon the birth of my two sons. After each son's birth came sly suggestions from my mother and/or grandmother about planning baptisms for each of them. In response, I quickly and succinctly shut them down again. My husband and I had always agreed we both felt the same way about formal religion. He was not really raised religiously, and we both decided, if our children wanted to explore religion later on, we would completely support that. But ultimately, it would be their choice and not ours.

Those baptism conversations with my mother and grandmother inevitably turned so very dark, with their predictions that my kids would end up in some sort of tumultuous afterlife that I didn't subscribe to, expressing sentiments I didn't teach to my kids, either. I have wanted them to map their own paths of spirituality in whatever direction they decide that they need, and I still do.

The third time this happened stuck with me like a tattoo. I was blessed to have the final moments with my sweet grandmother before she passed away while in hospice care. I tried to spend as much time as I could with her. I knew that it was a true blessing to be with her at the end of her precious life. I will get to her at another time. But it is no understatement to say here that true Irish women are forces to be reckoned with, and she was no exception.

I spent time with her by the hospice bed, washing her face and hair, putting lotion on her hands and feet, and getting her the best snacks or basically anything else she wanted. I put my own emotions on a serious pause, because I needed to. In crises and medical emergencies, I am able to be as calm as a cucumber.

Shortly before she passed away, my grandmother asked me if I would reconsider baptizing my boys, so she could "at least" see them in the afterlife. I didn't respond. I figured it was better than lying to her on her literal death bed.

I am a parent of two boys raised in our agnostic home, and they do not burst into flames when they enter a church. (Although years ago, my oldest son, while acting as the ring bearer at my brother-in-law's wedding, asked me what a "church" was, upon entering one for their ceremony. Maybe there needs to be a better balance? We shall see.)

I do want to share some true nuggets that my sweet grandmother left me or taught me, plus other indelible memories of her.

She was eighteen years younger than my grandfather, and no one ever really gave this a second thought.

She was kind. I mean, *the kindest*. I can still hear her distinctive laugh. My brother and I can do a wonderful impression of her, but it's only funny to those who were lucky enough to know her.

She took care of my cousins with every ounce of love she could muster. And in return, my cousins cared for her in many ways, especially after my dear grandfather passed away. I will introduce you to the man, the myth, the legend, Michael Killeen, later: he gets and deserves his own section.

She drank bourbon, gambled often as they lived in Las Vegas, and hit more royal flushes than anyone I know. This is still a point of contention with my husband, who loves to play poker and gamble. I revel in reminding him on occasion that, although he may have bad luck sometimes when he gambles, I know someone who had the best luck. (Although, once time, my husband overserved her bourbon in my kitchen, and we had to call for an ambulance.)

When she moved to be closer to my mother and aunt in Colorado, she had "companions" at her new living facility. Multiple male friends with whom she would dine with and spend time. She wasn't shy about it, nor did she want my mom *not* to have companions of her own, after she divorced my father. But only once my mother felt she was ready.

She loved driving her enormous Crown Victoria, even when we were the unfortunate, terrified passengers. She loved Red Lobster and pizza, and she made every single one of her children, grandchildren, and great-grandchildren feel special and loved.

Shortly before she passed away, she told me not to worry, because worrying is praying for something that you don't want. To this day, I still say this to my kids, friends, and whoever needs to hear it.

At her memorial service, cards were passed out with the following saying:

LET'S RESOLVE:

To be a little better
Than we have been before.
To be a little kinder
And to smile a little more.
To go about our living
With a firm hold on our nerve,
And to be a little wiser
As our judgments we reserve.
To be a little blinder
To things that hurt our pride,
To be a little calmer
And take life in our stride.
To be a little gentler
No matter how we feel,
That is the way we can all
Make happiness come real.

I hope that whoever is reading this is equally blessed with someone in their life like my sweet Grandma Anne. Someone who, without even trying, becomes a North Star for those who need it. Who shows endless grace, kindness, love, and humor in life's best and worst of times. Who is, quite honestly, one of the best human beings I have ever met.

I am honored to have had the privilege of being part of her life. Personally, I consider myself a lucky Irish girl for having her in my life. I will forever feel her presence and love.

The Layers in our Eyes

My eyes have three different colors in them. On a normal day, they are green and blue, a perfect combination of my mother (Irish green) and my father (blue on the outside). But when placed under bright light, my eyes are brown around my pupil, green around that, and blue on their outer edges.

I used to think they were strange and different. I now know I was blessed with these eyes. They are part of who I am. I know they are unique. I know they are beautiful. I often examine them at night. In front of my mirror, I tend to stare into them deeply. Sometimes, I will reflect on my day when I gaze at them. Other times, I will reflect on memories that give me pause, in order to see how I feel about them at that moment and to consider how I responded to them before and afterward. I do not always reflect on things with sadness or regret. Sometimes, it is with measured honesty and appreciation. In those times, I find gratitude.

I started to think about eyes tonight and realized how, if you look deep enough, you can see the layers of people and of yourself within your eyes. The profound green is the part I earned proudly from my mom and maternal family. That green has continued, albeit in different shades and tones, through my aunts, my cousins, their children, and mine.

I had never thought about it much before, but what a remarkable thing green eyes are. I know, if you study the science and genetics of it all, you can explain the rarity of green eyes. And that rarity is not lost on me, now that I am older. But what I know better is how this eye color represents my familial connection, which is something I truly treasure.

The blue ring around my green eyes comes directly from my blue-eyed dad. They are blue like Paul Newman's. For me, depending on the light hitting them, the blue can be overshadowed by the green in my eyes. But in the right light, the blue is beautiful and makes my eyes pop like you couldn't believe. Or so says my husband.

And then there's the brown. In bright light, the brown color is bright and vivid. My brother shares these same green eyes. We have very similar faces, yet our eyes are somewhat different. He has one green eye that is also half-brown. It started as a small spot and then it grew and grew, until the color overtook one half of his eye. Not quite a "David Bowie" with two different colored eyes, but pretty damn close. I think it is quite cool, honestly.

Growing up, we used to joke how many times people would look at him and say, "Oh, wow. Did you know one of your eyes is half-brown and green?"

He would respond with something sarcastic and clever, like, "No way! You are kidding!" As if he'd survived for his whole life without looking in a mirror. I always felt a bit envious of that cool trait he was blessed with. It makes him unique and special.

It's crazy, but now I often think about things like this in really metaphoric ways. My brother and I share very similar faces, but we are really different people. And yet, given the right circumstances, we are also very much the same. We share inside jokes, both have wickedly dry senses of humor, and find hilarity in examining the stupid and ironic things in our lives. I guess siblings are often similar like this.

I love my brother, even when we disagree or argue. Even when we are both fallible. Despite all of that, he is a testament to everything that is possible. And despite, when he was a difficult teenager, people telling him it was unlikely he would become anything, he is opinionated while being funny as hell. He can be stoic, sometimes cold, and often indifferent. But he loves his life, his wife, and his children fiercely and has worked his ass off to get there. He is successful. Did I mention he is funny and clever?

He is my only brother. I deeply wish we could connect more sometimes, but as I grow older, I understand that what I have is a brother, and that is enough. As an adult child with older parents, I will be forever grateful for traveling through this journey of life with him, to have him to lean on during all of the responsibilities and difficulties we have encountered as our parents get older. I am so grateful to not travel these roads alone.

When I was deciding whether or not to have more than one child in our family, I found myself unsure whether I wanted to do it all over again, and I searched out reasons why I should or should not have another baby. We hear a million times how hard it is to have your first baby. And yes, for us, too, it was all new and exciting to be first-time parents. But it was also so incredibly hard for me, as a mom, to figure it all out.

Spoiler alert: *no one* has it all figured out the first time around. I had a beautiful newborn baby boy with enormous brown eyes and a penchant for not sleeping, who screamed for hours due to colic and needed to be in constant motion. In the midst of my vexing decision around doing it all over again, my own parents were neck-deep in their own divorce. And they were in the midst of the worst parts of divorce—money, fighting, separate living situations... You get the picture.

I remember clearly thinking how this would be exponentially more awful if I had to do this by myself. *That* was the deciding factor to have two children instead of one. In hindsight, I cannot fathom life without my two boys. But at the time, the definitive and deciding factor for me, what greenlit the idea of having a sibling for my son, came after I really, deeply thought about my first son.

God forbid something would happen to my marriage or to my husband or me. Or if anything bad were to happen, really, if he had to carry that burden on his shoulders by himself, it just seemed like an untenable ask. Truly, it would end up being a burden on him, one he'd never have asked for or deserved. Isn't it strange how desperately you want to insulate your children from life's difficulties, even before they are even born?

My parents' divorce was rough, no doubt about it. There were money issues, there were health issues, there were addiction issues, and there was a complete and total disconnect between the two of them. And although my brother and I may never see their split in the same way, (though I really wish we could), we did lean into each other. As best we could, we tried to manage the chaos that arose out of their demise. I do think my brother lucked out, winning with the bigger piece of the wishbone, when he went to college out of state and was able to escape their split. Not that it was his intention, but I think he was just luckier than I was in that situation.

Eventually, I learned about all of my parents' ugly truths. Each in their own way admitted to me some of their individual and joint decisions. The hardest part of their breakup was watching their contempt for each other grow and grow. It was quite obvious, despite their attempts to mask it. At first, in private, each parent made mild disparaging comments to me about the other. And eventually, they didn't even try to keep it hidden. Things became uncomfortable between them, and I was in between them, as an unwilling referee. So, it was really nice to have my brother to talk to about all this.

As we have grown older, my feelings have changed, as have his. My brother and I are able to have discussions about both of our parents—sometimes, just basic information, superficial; but sometimes it is deep. Either way, to this day, we still see some things in a different way. And I recognize now how those differences are okay, a blessing, actually. When I was younger, our differences often felt like an afront to my observations and opinions, at the time. Now, however, I see this as my needing to examine things, like their divorce, from all angles.

I remain extremely proud of what my brother has accomplished. At times, it is hard not to see him as that flailing high school (almost) dropout, but he is *not* that at all. He beat the expectations of the "professional" counselors and teachers who wrote him off as a troubled teen more likely to succeed in less professional arenas. I think his big "fuck you" to those people is one of the things I admire most. For me, there's nothing more satisfying than my own "fuck yous" to people, situations, or decisions I have made that were not expected of me.

I don't know if these feelings and thoughts about my brother will ever change, or if they are "healthy" or not. I have an unending need for his love, approval, and recognition, things I don't even ask for from my own parents. I desperately wish my brother and I could lower our defenses and be unabashedly honest; could laugh until we cried all at our old jokes and just be okay. No judgment, no opinions about each other's decisions. Just unconditional love from my big brother. I don't know if that will ever come. I am not blameless in this situation, but I do think I try. And he does, too, in his own way. There is peace in that, as well.

I hope someday, when my sons are older, they will lean into each other, too. I hope they will have each other to bounce ideas off of and can soldier through, together, when their dear parents become difficult and unbearable. I hope they will appreciate that the greatest gift they have is each other—even when they succumb to anger or frustration with each other.

When they would fight when they were younger, I often told them to remember they each have only one brother. *One.* And they can either destroy each other or love each other. They are each other's greatest resource and blessing.

I love when I catch them making silly inside jokes to each other, knowing that neither their dad nor I have any idea what they are talking about. Or when they take the blame for each other.

When they are being each other's biggest cheerleaders, there is a little blow to my heart sometimes, because they remind me of my brother. I am so very grateful to have him. And I hope he feels the same way about his little sister.

Loss

Loss is an overwhelming concept. It can refer to losing my favorite shoes. Or when I lost my keys. *Or* when I lost track of where I was headed. And I know I've lost my own vision for my future self, lost myself, at times, something I realized after time passed. Sometimes it felt like I lost myself just for the sake of my marriage. Sometimes, for the sake of my family or friends. I think the most profound loss was losing myself for the sake of everyone else around me.

This book took a short hiatus, a needed break for me to regroup. I wasn't entirely sure I even wanted to continue writing. I pressed those around me about the indelicate truths of what I was writing about, and I ended up receiving a much less positive reception than I had hoped for. I was grief-stricken, as a result. Before asking, I had believed, no matter whom I spoke to, they would be utterly supportive of my project, sharing a basic understanding that this was a wonderfully cathartic, positive, and eye-opening experience for me, to write this *all* down.

But life had other plans. Besides polling my dearest friends, I was finally confronted by those people who willfully opposed my continuing to write this book. I honored their feelings because I felt I should. I stopped writing so as to not hurt any other people, again because I felt I should. I took the side of the naysayers and stopped, as it felt like the right thing, what I *should* do.

But there is that word again. *Should.* Who defines "should"? Is it those in your innermost circle who know you, know your foibles and flaws and can hold a well-formed opinion about you? I would caution you to take those opinions as just that. Opinions are not tried-and-true facts. There are opinions everywhere. Like an asshole, we all have one. I have come to understand that others' opinions belong to them. Not to you.

During my book-writing hiatus, I took a good, hard, and uncomfortable look at those opinions. Even before submitting the manuscript to a total stranger, I realized the ripple effect my words might have on others. On my husband, on my children, on my friends and family. Do those opinions decide what road *you* should take? No. I most certainly know this for sure. I believe, if you flip that opinion on its head, it forces the person who deflected it onto you to look at themselves. And for me, that was definitely an unwanted and unwarranted thing. Their discomfort is transferred to you, and you do not deserve to have it.

Initially, the anger, frustration, excuses, etc. come fast and furious from those people. At least in my experience, it definitely did. But I have now learned that it isn't for forever. And even if it is, that is their decision and not mine.

Shortly before my first manuscript deadline, I looked into my bathroom mirror and asked myself if I really wanted to do this. Did I really wanted to show the world my faults and those of my family and friends? Every time I asked myself those questions, my first instinctual answer was always *yes*! Yes to showing flaws, yes to showing reality, and yes to showing that being a real human isn't the worst thing in the world.

Then I took stock of the people I loved and cared about, and I realized the common denominator in each and every person I kept close to my heart was their being viciously honest in their own lives, and I utterly adore that trait. I realized that how they felt about our friendships and relationships revealed their own humanity, without any shame. So, I decided not to stop but to continue onward.

I have talked with my kids about these feelings in themselves and those around them. We have talked about weathering the storm of other people's opinions and intentions. No matter how hard you try, you really can never make decisive choices, if you filter then first through the opinions of other people. It is far easier for others to have divisive opinions of *your* life and to remain untainted by their own decisions in their own lives. If people took their magnifying glass and turned it around to view their own life decisions, however, chances are they would not always like or agree with what they see. I think that idea really resonated with my sons. At least, I hope it did.

So, instead of giving up on this book and shelving it forever, I decided to pivot in order to reflect the real reason I started writing in the first place. I hope this gives others the grace to fall and to utilize other people's mistakes and missteps to learn and grow. I hope people can learn from my mistakes and perhaps do something different as a result.

I fervently hope I can help others develop a skill-set that offers them that ability and appreciation to fail. To fall. To change who they are, and to recognize those around them who are unwilling to support their path. And that is so A-OK.

The reality of it all is that I have been, and likely always will be, attracted to the people who were once broken; who have acknowledged it, learned from it, and then became their best selves. I know I will lose people around me as a result. That foul or yellow card, if you will, will likely be called on me from time to time. Bring it on.

But let's also be honest about that. How often do you call "foul" on yourself? In your darkest moments, when you are trying to hold it all together. I know my own pattern. I used to call foul when I was so sure that I could point out the misgivings of other people around me. Wow! What a helpful tool to validate my own poor decisions! I wouldn't have done that if *they* hadn't… blah, blah, blah: insert blaming statement right here. You can really master the art of deflecting your own responsibility, if you are skilled and try to make others feel responsible for your bad choices.

Don't get me wrong. I know this is far easier to say when you're on the outside, looking in. I mean, who really likes someone who points out, with accuracy and most likely evidence, that you are flawed. It hurts a lot.

For me, it is mainly because I have always felt powerless to change whatever flaws I could still fervently argue I had. I used the excuse that my flaws were just simply a part of me, like it or not.

Until I didn't feel that way anymore, and I didn't think that way anymore, either.

My Grandfather

My maternal grandfather, Michael Killeen, left Ireland on the *USS Baltic* and landed on Ellis Island on September 24, 1922. He moved from Ireland to the United States on his own. He was a stoic, strong, and patriarchal figure in my family's life. I don't know how to emphasize the enormous impact he has had on the maternal side of my family. The stories about him have reached such amazing, maybe hyperbolic levels, they may all be true, though some may be fiction! Regardless, his impact on my life and on my maternal cousins' lives, my mother's and her sisters' lives, and most certainly on my dear late grandmother's life, has been so palpable and noteworthy, I feel Grandpa Mike deserves his own story here.

As I mentioned, my grandfather was eighteen years older than my grandmother. He was born in 1904, and she was born in 1922. Although I assume it gave some people reason to pause, it never seemed to be an issue in our family. My grandparents were incredibly loving people who helped family members in Chicago after they were married; they also helped their own extended family and my cousins immensely, too.

In my recollection, my grandfather was stern and had the strongest handshake of anyone I have ever met. To many other people, in his later years, he was a grumpy and demanding old man who had extensive expectations of any restaurant we went to. He often made strange demands of the wait staff at restaurants, asking for his favorite things. He always had to have a side of sour cream, regardless of what he was eating, oftentimes as a palate cleanser or even a dessert. That would often throw the wait staff wherever we were off, but they would try their best to accommodate his wishes.

He also carried half-and-half in his pocket, to ensure he had one additional thing he loved with every meal. And he always supplied that himself, if need be. He also had high expectations of restaurants and their food, because he had worked as a chef himself in Chicago when my mom and her sisters were little.

He was a chef at the Standard Club, a Chicago supper club long ago. In my mind, I always pictured the supper club as a place of extremely frivolous people eating and drinking extravagant food and drinks, a place frequented by some unsavory people, as well as successful ones. I do not believe I am very far off in my imagination.

My mother told me many stories about my grandfather, who always worked late and often through holidays, leaving them home until he was done at work. She mentioned to me that one or more of the patrons of the club had felt guilty for keeping my Grandpa Mike at work and away from his own family, so they provided a Christmas tree to her family, to make things easier. Occasionally, these wealthy supper-club members paid for a holiday dinner for my mother's family or offered them other things to make up for my grandfather's absence. When we were older, my mom explained how it was *highly* likely that some of the fellas at the supper club were not earning their living in legally acceptable ways.

When they married, my mother and father were gifted furniture for their first home from the Standard Club—a couch, dressers, table, and nightstands. My mom worked at the Standard Club while going to college in Chicago. The club also had apartments on the upper floors for its members. The fourth floor was the men's floor, and in order to deliver menus to those residents, my mother would ride the elevator up but wasn't allowed to leave the cab to deliver them to the men living there.

She would often share memories of her upbringing and life with her extremely large Irish family in Chicago. At one point, she and her parents lived in her grandparents' tiny Chicago apartment. A total of sixteen people were living in that apartment, with all of the kids sleeping on fold-away cots in the living room or dining room, lined up like a hospital ward.

My mom also described how my great-grandmother, Great-grandma Gallagher, welcomed, housed, fed and clothed all of their extended family whenever she needed to, as best as she could. I was lucky enough to meet and get to know my great grandmother during her final years in Las Vegas, albeit briefly. My mother described her as the quintessential matriarchal figure in my mother's family. Therefore, my own grandmother and grandfather's feelings about helping care for family makes total sense.

My oldest maternal cousin, one of several cousins who were closely supported by my grandparents as they were growing up, decided to make it her work to learn and find out the details of our family history, heritage, and lineage. And all of us cousins on my maternal side are incredibly grateful that she put in the time, effort, and knowledge to learn about our family.

Here is what I know about my grandfather, things I hope are inspiration and directives for my own life.

My grandfather lived in a small house in Ireland that had dirt floors and lacked working indoor plumbing. There are still people who reside in his village in Ireland who remember my grandfather and his family and tell stories about him. Luckily, my cousin found these people and developed a connection, so more than one of my maternal cousins has met them, while visiting Ireland. I hope to do the same someday.

Village folklore has it that my grandfather was supposed to be on the maiden voyage of the *Titanic*, but, according to Irish tradition, it is bad luck to be on the maiden voyage of a ship, he decided not to go. I believe he followed his instincts, which, over and over again, proved to be a reliable guide for him.

After my grandfather landed at Ellis Island as an Irish immigrant, he was entirely on his own and had to make his way in the world. He worked in a grocery store and lived with his sister in New York City. We have a wonderful picture of him standing in front of that store. Also, rubbings of the brick with his name, which the family commissioned to honor him, when Ellis Island was renovated several years ago

I recall his ridiculously strong handshake and even stronger resolve, which came, I believe, from his start in the world. In his culinary career, I recall visiting him as child and watching him sharpen his knives all the time, working with his hands each and every day. His hands were those of a brave man and seasoned chef who would tolerate nothing but the best in the world from his food and from his company. As I said before, this is likely why his ranted sometimes to unwitting, vulnerable wait staff during his visits to restaurants or why his demands seemed completely acceptable to waitstaff. Still, when my dear Grandpa Mike would complain about the food, the service, or whatever else seemed unacceptable to him, my mother and father would look at each other and turn completely red or pale in embarrassment.

All his quirks aside, the funniest thing I remember about my grandfather was how, despite his hardened demeanor, he loved all of his daughters and grandchildren fiercely. I mean, do *not* mess with Michael Killeen, or you will get the receiving end of his indignation and anger. And his reactions came from a place of complete and utter refusal to deviate from his own opinion, as well as from a genuine place of love. Mind you, if you crossed him or made him angry, he had no problem telling you so—even if you *were* his daughter or grandchild.

One of my most lasting memories of Grandpa Mike was from one of my last visits with my brother and family in Las Vegas. My grandparents moved to Las Vegas in

1978 and loved the climate, the gambling, and their life there. During this particular trip, I remember spending days with my cousins at their home, playing in their pool all day long. My brother and I thought that spending a day at a house with a pool was *so* glamorous and enviable.

Afterward, my brother and I returned to our grandparents' house for dinner. When we entered their home, my grandfather was sharpening his knives rapidly, wearing his "Kiss the Chef" apron. While he aggressively sharpened those blades, my stoic grandfather told me we were having spaghetti for dinner and also mentioned, in no uncertain terms, that if we didn't like spaghetti, we would go hungry that night. That was how Grandpa Mike was: kind as an angel, loving as anyone, but I also would not cross him for anything.

I hope my boys have those kinds of memories about their parents and grandparents. I hope our own stories offer both of them the foundation to understand legacies and memories. I am eternally grateful for my own extended family, who have taught me, my brother, and my cousins about our own history. I hope my boys feel the same way about their own crazy parents.

Mainly, I hope our own stories and experiences, those I have already shared with my boys and the ones they may learn from reading this book, offer them the opportunity to use our experiences and past decisions to season their own decisions as they grow up.

Partying

When I was sixteen years old, we teenagers were fortunate to have "all-ages" dance clubs in Colorado. We could go to clubs within thirty minutes of our house or to ones hours away, depending on the day of the week.

My group and I made every effort to go to each and every one. I had a cohort who joined me and/or drove me everywhere. We would leave our house at 11 p.m. and drive to Boulder. I went to more fraternity parties in my teens than I ever did as a college-aged person, mainly, I think, because my friends and I were reliving our deep appreciation for the movie *Heathers,* each and every time.

We were avid partiers. I cannot stress that enough. I would drive *anywhere* for a party, for drinks and drugs, and to hang out with friends. I always assumed I would return home safe afterward, regardless of the company I was keeping. My companions, though, sometimes were not as interested in self-preservation and making it home safely.

Sometimes, we drove for almost two hours, from our side of town all the way to Boulder, to see what these fraternity parties were all about, following our *Heathers* mentality and need for taking our rightful place at college parties. We had a resilient and reckless attitude, with not a care in the world.

I know I have mentioned these things to my own children on occasion, but I am doubtful they understood the gravity of what we were doing. I willingly participated in so many dangerous situations and barely escaped and/or survived, a fact that is difficult for me to admit or to reconcile with what I try to teach my kids today.

One day, my son asked about the times when my husband and I were younger, wondering what we did when we went to parties. What, exactly, were we up to, way back when? The truth is, I haven't told him everything, and I probably never will. I realize now that he has started to accumulate his own secrets and his own experiences. I wonder if he already has similar profound memories that will stay with him for his lifetime, like mine have. As a parent, I sometimes carry almost excessive worry about what he is up to, like all parents of teenagers. Even though he will throw me an over-the-top eye roll whenever I question his decisions, ask him about his life, or still try to remain relevant in his eyes.

I do feel lucky that I chose not subscribe to every rule, expectation, and consequence I was raised with. Not that I think it is necessarily a bad thing, but I do know the difference, and I do not try to force shame on my son. And more important, I do not ignore him. Our conversations are real, frank, embarrassing, and hilariously honest.

A few months ago, we were talking about sex, girlfriends, and life, and he looked at me and thanked me and his dad. When I asked what he was thanking us for, he replied that he knows, no matter what he tells us, we will listen. And he knows that there is no need to lie and no need to worry, because he knows we just love him for being our son.

If I am being honest, I really hope he harbors *some* secrets and that those secrets are planted within as seeds for his own personal growth. Maybe some are mortifying. Most definitely, some are intense. Others will keep him honest and real with himself and his friends.

His dad and I have briefly mentioned some of the more notable events during our "heavier" partying days while growing up. The following are some of the best nuggets we shared, so our son can carry pieces of our youthful experiences as he begins to make his own crazy memories.

When we were freshmen in high school, white supremacists and white nationalists ran rampant in my part of Colorado. I cannot explain why, but probably it was due to the gothic-style club culture and parties I went to with my friends. In hindsight, I can see how that racist ideology attracted people easily drawn toward their darker sides.

I am somewhat ashamed to admit that, while I never subscribed to their beliefs, these supremacist guys were welcomed at many, if not most, of the parties and dance clubs I went to. People's houses I frequented also saw these skinheads show up or they would be there already, when I arrived.

While I was frankly terrified of them all, I was also fascinated by them, as well. I never witnessed any of them become violent exercising their "beliefs" or exhibiting criminal behavior. But the rumors about what they had either done or might do, if provoked, swirled around our crowd. On a few occasions, while hanging out in random houses, I noticed these guys' propensity for drugs, weapons, and graffiti, and observed their love of violence, which was likely to manifest itself somewhere and with someone very unlucky soon.

One afternoon, during my free period/lunch hour at school, I ended up in the spray-painted basement of an apartment that didn't seem to belong to any actual adult. It was about 11:45 in the morning, and there were cigarettes and joints burning in an ashtray while music blared. On another grossly dirty table across the basement were even more cigarettes, empty beer bottles, a few knives, and random bullets.

A few of the "gentlemen" in the basement wore Doc Martens with their laces laced straight across, which I found ironic, since this particular color and style of lacing meant they were considered "straight-edge" skinheads who were not interested in using drugs or alcohol. In hindsight, I highly doubt that was true.

Then there was the glossary of the *kinds* of laces people put in their boots. White laces = White Nationalist/White Power. Red laces = Neo Nazi/fascist assholes that you didn't want to mess with. Black laces (like the original ones that came with the boots) = straight-edged or non-conforming to a group. Yellow laces = anti-racist. And there was a plethora of other groups, and a plethora of lacing styles that indicated different things. As of late, there are more colors that mean even *more* different things, but those were the main ones I knew of, at that time.

It was interesting how this particular group of skinheads claimed to encourage being violent toward people they despised, but God forbid they, themselves, would admit to drinking a beer or smoking a joint, even though they did.

I left and went back to school that day, returning home to my suburban life with my suburban family. Truth be told, I ended up feeling exhilarated and terrified at the same time.

Those delightful fellas from that disgusting basement ended up frequenting *many* of the parties and clubs I went to with my group of friends. With their skinhead jackets with stupid sewn-on patches, their stupid white nationalist band T-shirts, and their shaved heads, they would appear at our dance clubs, our parties, our coffee houses—basically everywhere. I still marvel at the fact that none of this seemed strange or scary to me at the time. Because it really, really, *really* should have. Maybe the fact that it didn't indicates my lack of awareness and inability to even recognize the red flags that should have been glaringly obvious.

During one party at Matt's home, in particular, one of these skinheads was parked in the dingy basement with a few others in his belligerent cohort, drinking, smoking, and doing God knows what else. By the time I arrived, the basement dwellers were completely wasted, high, and extremely obnoxious. Their conversations began to become more and more based around violence.

I became very nervous listening to their desire to hurt anyone around them, specifically anyone from any race other than their own. I had never really thought anything would ever even come of their comments, just that they were stupid, bored suburban kids subscribing to something they didn't and couldn't actually believe in. At the time, I thought they were interested in white supremacy as a result of the music we all were listening to. I heard about some of the skinheads' fights with people on the weekends, though I was never sure if these stories were true or not. As it turned out, they were *very* true.

I'm not sure how long it was after that basement party when I was shaken by the news that these guys caused a racist disruption with a Black person during either a party or a concert. I had heard they started a fight with the Black man and beat him pretty viciously. Shortly thereafter, a "rematch" was proposed for them all to meet up and beat the shit out of each other yet again.

It was to this second altercation that a gun was brought to what was basically a knife-and-fist fight. The Black victim of the first beating became one of the perpetrators of violence during the final fight, where the skinhead I knew was fatally shot. I do not know the legal outcome of any of that, but I do know I was shaken from those events. I wanted to put as much distance between me and those people as possible. After all, what would it take for these altercations to repeat themselves at any given party where I was present? It would take very little.

There was another fella in our circle of friends who subscribed to the majority of skinhead ideals, but who was absolutely hilarious and fun to be around. And, funny story, he was Black! I know that sounds absurd, but he was the most *individual* person. He held his ideals tightly and appreciated the confusion others had toward his seemingly conflictual beliefs. Back in the day, I think he kind of reveled in that dichotomy.

Once I got over my own initial questions about him, I absolutely fell in love with his personality. He loved the same kind of music we all did, he could make you laugh like no other, and he went to the same dance clubs we all flocked to. As you can imagine, he became quite legendary in our city.

There was a huge house party at our friend's home that had gotten completely out of control. Matt's parents were out of town, and when we arrived, the interior of their house appeared to have exploded. There were people everywhere: in the basement, the living room, the backyard, and all the way up through the house and into his parents' bedroom. Everyone in the house was clearly drunk or high or both.

But don't get me wrong—this was a ridiculously fun party. Dana and I drank, danced, and laughed for hours. Matt, the "host" of the party, and his older brother had weathered their own teenage storms with their two parents in recent years. Dana was even treated by Matt's parents as one of their children, and often stayed at their house to avoid his own house. He felt loved and comfortable there.

Unfortunately, Matt's mother was suffering from cancer at the time and had a collection of wigs in her bedroom. Dana and I decided to head upstairs to make out. Our African-American skinhead friend put on one of her blonde wigs and dance around the bedroom, making me laugh so hard I needed a bathroom. It was such a fun night…, until it wasn't.

Suddenly, I heard yelling and screams from downstairs. At first, I thought people were screaming as they listened to music and danced. Quickly, I realized there was nothing joyful or positive about those screams. A large fight with uninvited people who were arriving had broken out inside the house. The shouts were telling them to leave, as they weren't welcome.

Apparently, they refused to go until the party guests started to hit them and kick them to get them to leave. We ran down the stairs to see what was going on. There was our wig-wearing friend dragging one of the unwanted guests out to the front lawn, screaming at him that he should have just left and now was going to regret that decision.

Our Black friend beat the intruder mercilessly, kicking him relentlessly in both his torso and his head. Mind you, as a "skinhead," he was also wearing traditional, steel-toed Doc Martens, forcing his boot down onto this uninvited guest's head. I immediately thought of the unforgettable scene from the movie *American History X*, where the head and mouth of the Black man was placed on the curb of their front lawn, while they kicked his head into the curb. The fight at this party held that kind of real estate in my mind, given its shocking level of violence. I had never seen anything like that before and thought it was only a matter of time before someone appeared with a gun.

It didn't take long for the police to arrive at the house. People inevitably scattered like mice upon their arrival, and those of us upstairs just hid around the house. Dana and I were hidden away in a closet/crawl-space in the master bedroom, praying that a police officer wouldn't find us. We waited until it sounded as though things had actually calmed down.

It had been quiet for a few minutes when we heard a loud, banging knock on the door. We both looked at each other, certain we were caught and would be graciously escorted by the police home.

Then, the door slowly opened, and a black, wig-wearing, skinhead screamed, *"Get outta there!"* I am hard-pressed to remember a time when I didn't laugh harder than that moment.

Fast forward a few years. I began out on my own in downtown Denver, starting at the ripe old age of seventeen. When I turned twenty-one, I was completely thrilled I would no longer need to fake my age in order to get into a bar.

My friend Kelly picked me up from my apartment to take me out to do some serious bar-hopping and dancing. The dancing part was not Dana's cup of tea, so it was just me and Kelly heading out on the town. By this time, every bar or club we went to had people whom either one or both of us knew.

The night of my twenty-first birthday *had* to be an amazing, right? I picked out the most amazing outfit for my special night, spending far more money than I probably should have. I paid extra attention to getting my makeup just right for the night. Basically, I paid extra, extra attention to all aspects of everything for my big night. After all, it was a milestone, and I wanted it to be as perfect as possible.

Our first stop was a well-known, well-established dance club called The Deadbeat Club. This was an infamous bar and club in Denver, one that most everyone I knew frequented. Some friends worked as bartenders there, while others worked as DJs.

We jumped into the club, immediately starting to dance and, more importantly, drink legally. Shortly thereafter, we made a beeline to the DJ booth, to say a quick hello to our friend, who was manning the turntables that night. Kelly informed him that we were there for my special night and requested a few special songs for the birthday girl.

He said he would oblige, and we headed to the bar to start the evening off right. We ordered some drinks and then a celebratory birthday shot. We were full of giggles and energy. Our DJ friend then loudly announced over the microphone that his friend, Erin, was there celebrating her twenty-first birthday. The club proceeded to sing "Happy Birthday" to me as the music stopped briefly. I thanked everyone in the club, and I thanked our friendly DJ, as well.

He immediately began to play one of the songs we had requested for our night. Kelly and I quickly left our drinks at the bar and bolted for the dance floor to laugh, sing, and dance. It felt magical. It was the kind of fun I had always hoped for.

After dancing to a few of the requested songs, we returned to the bar to finish our drinks and to figure out where our next stops would be that evening. We danced there a little bit more, but then I started to feel sick. It was a strange kind of sickness that didn't feel at all normal to me.

Spoiler alert: I was obviously well-aware of what it felt like for me to be drunk, even *really* drunk. I knew what my drinking limits were and, more important, when to stop very early on. But this was a different kind of drunk and a very different kind of "sick." It came on really fast. I looked at Kelly and told her I thought I should probably go home. I know she was somewhat disappointed, as she'd also had high hopes for the night. But she obliged, and we walked out of the club toward her car. That was the last thing I remember.

I woke up completely naked under a thin blanket and sheet, and I couldn't speak. I quickly realized that a tube had been put down my throat. I began to panic. As I began to come to a bit more, I grabbed the tube and tried to pull it out of my esophagus while choking uncontrollably.

A nurse darted to my bed, grabbed my arms, and held me down while the professionals quickly removed the tube themselves. Everything still appeared blurry to me, and I was completely confused.

The tube leaving my throat so rapidly felt like someone was scraping their fingernails up from the center of my body until it finally came out. I was terrified. I didn't know where I was, how I'd gotten there, or what had actually happened to me.

Dana was at my side, in tears, immediately telling me how scared he was. He hugged me, kissed me, and then just held me. After a few moments, I asked the nurse who'd removed the tube what was going on.

The nurse proceeded to tell me I had had "a little too much fun on my twenty-first birthday," insinuating that I must have had alcohol poisoning from excessive drinking. But that didn't make any sense to me at all.

After a few more minutes, as I pieced together what was happening, it was clear that the nurse's bedside manner was severely lacking. Dana had brought clothes to the hospital that I could change into, when I was finally able to leave. Leaving the emergency room, as I walked past the nurses' station, they sarcastically began to sing "Happy Birthday to me as I walked out. It was utterly embarrassing, humiliating, and confusing.

When I sat in the car with Dana, he explained what had happened after everything went black as I walked to Kelly's car the night before. Kelly had been equally confused by my reaction that night.

I asked her to drive me home, placed my head out the passenger window as we drove, and became violently sick over and over again. Kelly told Dana I had attempted to talk to her in the car, but my words didn't make sense and were out of order, and I eventually fell asleep in the front seat on the way to my apartment.

She brought Dana downstairs to help carry me upstairs. He asked Kelly how I had become so badly drunk, but then he quickly realized he needed to call for an ambulance for me, as my breathing began to grow slower and stranger, until it seemed to start and then stop. When the ambulance arrived at our apartment, they intubated me on the sidewalk in front of my apartment, quickly cutting off my precious new outfit right there, in front of my neighbors, before taking off to Denver General Hospital. Dana told me it was terrifying. To him, it was abundantly clear I had been drugged at the club, but that he didn't know what I was given. I'd appeared basically dead by the time I was brought home.

Prior to the snarky chorus of nurses singing me out of the emergency room, we did ask a nurse to test my blood, so we could know what drug I had been given. I really wanted to know for sure. But each nurse repeatedly refused, again chalking up my condition to being an overindulgent, new twenty-one-year-old girl.

After that experience, Dana and I sat at our kitchen table trying to wrap our heads around what had just happened. I had widely advertised my birthday to a club full of predators without even knowing it. The only thing I really came away with from our conversation was how grateful we both were that he was so quick to recognize I wasn't okay, when I'd returned home. We were both even more grateful that he knew me so well that he could recognize these bizarre symptoms.

Since that birthday, overindulging for me can be difficult, especially if I am not safely in my home. That feeling of losing control of my surroundings can immediately put me into a fight-or-flight mode. I am forty-seven years old now, and I *still* have the same response. The human condition to protect yourself when you sense the need to is remarkable, really. It is difficult to accept the fact that there are people in this world who ultimately are not looking out for your best interests. Rather, they have something far more sinister in mind.

Lately, my oldest son and his friends have been partaking in partying much more. And to be honest, I absolutely love that they are doing it now. Unlike my own parents, I think this is where and when you earn your salt, and kids can learn so much about themselves, their friends, and their own lives. I hope they learn to revel in the unpredictability of having one plan at 8:00 p.m., another one at 9:00 p.m., and inevitably another at 11:00 p.m.

But do not mistake this for me identifying myself as the "fun mom" who has no rules, limits, or boundaries. That is surely not the case with yours truly. I am a firm believer in utilizing these situations to learn about yourself, for meeting a partner and making history and memories. Most importantly, it helps with figuring out who you actually are. So, in that vein, I do encourage my sons to "party." They can experiment, learn, grow, and also be safe at the same time. Hiding my sons from bad experiences and pretending those experiences do not exist is not realistic. I will continue to have the difficult conversations with my kids, because pretending those conversations aren't needed just does not make any sense to me.

Recently, my oldest son went to a noteworthy party with some of his high school friends. It was a crazy experience that left him shaken, literally, as the floor of the party house collapsed due to the weight of the 150-plus kids present and bouncing around on the floor. By God's good graces, no one was killed. But it caused tremendous trauma for my son, the friend with him, and all of the other kids who were there at the time.

Although there were parents and other adults present at the time, this particular party had become completely out of control, and the authorities were called to try to intervene. I happened to be out of town that night, but social media made it impossible for me *not* to learn about this even before I could return to Colorado. I was absolutely terrified for my son, of course, but also terrified for all of the other kids and adults who were present at the party. And boy, my son was shaken from that night.

Eventually, I was able to speak with him, stupidly trying to hide my parental fear of what could have happened to him. He tried to reassure me that he was fine, but he wasn't. He was also certain that someone surely had been killed by the collapse, and that realization left him in tears. I think that night was the only time I was grateful for Snapchat, social media, and my parental pipeline that supplied me with the play-by-play of the evening.

After some time had passed and I'd had a chance to reflect, I realized how many times I had nearly been hurt and/or killed—more than I should have allowed myself to be. Growing up, how many times had I dodged fate's bullet while out "partying" with my friends? Whether it was driving when we shouldn't have been driving anywhere, going to places where we surely didn't belong, or otherwise making piss-poor decisions all under the guise of a good time.

I like to think that my oldest son is reliving my own partying anthology in all its glory. I just pray that he uses these situations to mold himself into the adult he can become and to learn from his own mistakes as well as the mistakes of others around him. God willing, without a criminal record or a life-threatening injury.

So let me get to my final point. Yes, this is my haphazard attempt to scare straight girls who unwittingly fall victim to the bar-crawling vermin out in the world. They do exist, they are real, and yes, this happens all the time.

But my bigger lesson from that experience is to pay attention. This is something I spoke with my son about, shortly after that floor-dropping party. I hope he has learned not to lose sight of your surroundings or of yourself. I hope my sons pay attention to those around them, and pay attention to things that may feel off in their gut. It doesn't have to be something with enormous consequences. Rather, it can be just the slightest thing that just doesn't feel quite right. It can be an oddly worded text message from a friend who may need their help. It can be the strange and oddly silent teenager in their midst.

But the most definite thing I hope they pay attention to is that little voice in your head that makes itself known to you from time to time. The voice that, for me, tells me when someone is walking behind me from a store, and it doesn't feel right. Or that voice that will tell me maybe someone in my life shouldn't be there anymore, because they aren't there for the right reasons. And, in light of the events listed above, I know I should have listened to myself and my own inner voice each and every time. I mean, we all really should stop and listen to that voice. For me, that inner voice—yep! That bitch definitely knows what she is talking about.

Sex

Sex. Doin' it. Intimacy. Fucking. Banging.

Quick question.... Were you raised talking about it? Because I wasn't. *Not at all.* A decent therapist worth their salt could tell you this is probably one of my biggest personal hang-ups. It's awkward when you are young. It's confusing, uncomfortable, and strange. Then there's the body of the other person. If you have never spoken the word (make sure you whisper this to maintain your decorum): *dick, penis, pecker, cock, Johnson, prick*!

Sex began with Dana. He was my first. He was sweet, gentle, and understanding. I am grateful the first time wasn't behind the school or in the back of his Toyota minivan. Turns out that was because I was *not* his first. Not even close. I was fifteen, and I lost my virginity on Mother's Day. I think there is some sort of symbolism there, but I won't stretch myself to search out the meaning. I mean, that's why I have paid good money to my many, many therapists over the years.

Circling back to my tendency to settle into autopilot more often than not, sex for us was no different. What *was* sexual pleasure? I didn't understand what that meant. Wasn't it just doing what he needed and/or wanted, in order to feel satisfied? Isn't that what a good girlfriend and future wife should do? I really had no clue. And most important, why did I feel so weird about sex, in general? I was certain my mom and dad had had sex. Well, at least twice. But I doubt much more than that.

Sex used to be very loaded for me. It carried with it shame and embarrassment and eventually brought feelings and memories from different relationships to the surface each and every time I had it. Then, the worst thing happened. It felt like another light-switch moment when I finally realized that, in many of my relationships, whenever I had sex with someone, it oftentimes was rape.

It still pains me to say that out loud, but it is just the truth, and you cannot sugarcoat it. Early on, I didn't know it was rape, except for on one occasion. I was with a particularly delightful fella just before I left for Europe, and he was keen on forceful and manipulative sex. He was even *more* keen on making me have sex when I was tired, when I didn't want to, and when I would say no.

Herein lies the epitome of my truth. I was raised to not cause problems; it has been my duty to take care of and fix my man. But with this guy, I had no idea what to do, how it should feel, and, most important, I didn't understand how to explain these confusing thoughts. And, fun fact, that particular ex-boyfriend's sister is a famous Hollywood actress who still is working and acting today, making it damn near impossible to avoid my memories of him, no matter how hard I try. And even when I travelled to another continent to escape them.

So, Dana received the blunt force trauma of my swirling insecurities, my flashbacks, and my ever-changing moods. It was horrible, and I wish I could have handled my past differently. We all have 20/20 hindsight when you've been dealt the hand of abuse. But it was far more confusing when I truly believed that relationship was normal, consensual, and loving.

I ended up shutting down, which was far safer than having to feel all of that every time we made love. Again, any half-witted therapist could tell you that a partner can be supportive, loving, and understanding for a while, but that cannot continue forever, especially if his needs are ignored for too long. Which is what I did. I am not proud, but I was in control, and I decided if, when, and how I wanted to be intimate. It was my call, which was what I really needed.

I eventually started to work with a therapist to excavate my personal scar tissue around sex and relationships. It took what felt like forever for me to be okay with intimacy. It took painstakingly deliberate attempts to chisel away at my scars. Prior to that, I would try to be "normal" when it came to sex, but I would inevitably end up in a panic-riddled puddle on the floor. I hated that feeling and am so grateful I do not feel like that anymore. I understand the undercurrents women feel about sex and their role in it. The spectrum of emotions attached to sex can be so very different for everyone.

Dana and I would break up and get back together over and over again. I used to be ashamed to admit it, but I overly compensated for my sexual insecurities by meeting man after man, stupidly believing, if I kept trying to figure this whole sex thing out, I would forget the horrible memories from my past. This, of course, never worked for me. I had to do the work and try to fix my heart and relearn how to love myself again.

Fast-forward to August 22, 2017. Discovering what my husband had been up to left me devastated. But if I am being honest, after some thought, I realized I truly wasn't surprised. In my screwed-up mind, I determined that he had gone from having a frigid wife to becoming Colorado's very own Hugh Hefner. Right? Isn't that what happens? I mean, if you are going to fuck over your wife, destroy your family, and possibly end your career, you might as well *really* blow your life up and go out *Jerry Maguire*-style. Mic drop. Adios.

Guess what? That isn't what happened, because I wouldn't let it. Don't get me wrong—I wanted to *and* I wanted to destroy him. Destroy all of those who enabled this to continue right in front of me without my knowledge. These supposed "friends" whom I found out were encouraging him to pursue this woman and leave me and our family. Those friends who lied to me so many times that I truly lost track.

I really wanted to destroy this woman, who had tried *way* too hard to be friends with me, to be close to me. Who would call and ask for advice about her young son. This woman who, I learned, had befriended my "friends," had worn my clothes, driven my car, and cried to me about her abusive ex-husband. Her performance was Oscar-worthy. I just wish I had paid better attention to what was right in front of my face. The signs were all there.

But I was watching my life unfold wearing glasses with the wrong prescription. Our life had become blurry and a self-propelled machine. The Hunts. The envied marriage and long relationship. We *were* the relationship goals for everyone we knew.

What does that say about me? I repeated that question in my head for months afterward. Years, truthfully. What else *didn't* I know? The questions and feelings of betrayal swirled, festered, and raised their ugly head explosively in different scenarios and situations.

I ended up with the seemingly right "glasses," eventually. And with those "glasses," I was certain that all men cheat. All of them. I would watch men suspiciously when I was at the gym, always convinced that each and every one of them was really just shopping for their next mistress. I think I substituted one pair of glasses with the wrong prescription for another with the wrong one, as well.

Speaking of the gym, I jumped into the deep end of working out. I figured, if I was going to be this angry, I might as well put it to good use. I worked out like a maniac. I later learned from friends at the gym that, during that time when I loved to slam medicine balls, punch boxing bags, and lift as much weight as I possibly could, I was terrifying to pretty much everyone there. I think this would explain why no one spoke to me: I was that crazy lady at the gym.

But it served its purpose for me. If I couldn't fix my heart or my mental health at that time, I might as well fix my body. Exercise has been such a blessing. It helped me immensely at that time. Now, I view it as something I am lucky enough to be able to do to the best of my ability. I mentioned I have two boys. But the truth is I have been pregnant more than twice. I have been pregnant more than three times. I carried such shame about this. Such shame in my behavior back then. (And despite this book's timing, I mention this not because of the abhorrent Supreme Court, although I would *love* to provide my own opinion about *that* shit show.)

The first time I mistakenly became pregnant, I was fifteen. It was reckless and irresponsible. I think I sat on the fence about whether or not to have a baby for about four minutes.

Termination was an awful but necessary experience. I somehow lied my way into the procedure and headed into the gate at Planned Parenthood. There were handfuls of people shaming and screaming at me with their hateful posters; at forty-seven, I still remember them clear as day. And their screaming threats *really* changed my mind right then and there… (Insert eye-rolling emoji here, along with a profoundly rigid middle finger.)

The best explanation I can give about why I made the decision I did was that it was the right decision for me and Dana. Period. I should also say, another underlying benefit of being raised by an Irish Catholic is that I can do a damn good job carrying tremendous guilt all by myself. Which is what I did. I didn't need strangers with megaphones and poorly worded signs screaming at me to make me feel awful. I was able to this perfectly well all by myself, thank you very much.

Sexually, I know I was reckless. Well, *we* were reckless. And I believe it had an awful lot to do with the fact that I had no idea what I was doing. I was always game and yet was *never* talked to about sex, the pitfalls, the medically necessary lessons, and the responsibility of having sex in general. I would often have pregnancy scares, and I really wish I had taken the time to better educate myself in sexual education. I navigated immature sexuality at my own peril. How I did not end up with more than just a few pregnancies is something I continue to feel embarrassed and ashamed about today. But I have already covered that topic.

Dana and I were married in 2002. Granted, for all intents and purposes, we had been married for *many* years prior to that. But, in the great state of Colorado, we tied the knot on June 22, 2002. In 2003, I became pregnant, and for the first time, after all of my haphazard pregnancy scares and irresponsible sexual escapades, I was *so* excited! I finally felt excitement for a positive pregnancy test, which was a new experience. Until then, it was always a shameful and cloudy "in memoriam" of past bad decisions and the foggy math that followed my late period. And the coolest thing about it was, this time, Dana was thrilled as well.

When I was about four months along, I went to visit my brother in Ohio, where he was living during his obstetrics residency. I went by myself, to spend quality time with him and his family and to take in *all* of the amazing highlights that Ohio had to offer.

We checked out a U2 exhibit at the Rock & Roll Hall of Fame in Cleveland, and while we were driving back to Canton in his Nissan Exterra, with its jolting manual transmission, I kept thinking, if I vomited in his car during this rough ride home, he would understand. He *really* knew all about women, especially pregnant ones.

Shortly before I was supposed to leave, we all went out to dinner, and I felt strange. As if I had chugged gallons of water without feeling full at all. I felt water seep down my leg at the restaurant table.

But it wasn't water. It was blood. In the bathroom, I discovered that the blood wouldn't stop and had stained my clothes. I briskly walked back to the table, pulled my brother aside, and said that something was very, very wrong. As per usual, my tears came fast and strong, and I was unable to hold myself together.

We spoke briefly at the table, quickly left the restaurant, and headed first to their house and then to the hospital where he worked. It was foggy, surreal, and terrifying. Not because I didn't know what was happening. In my heart, I already knew. But because I knew I would have to call my new husband and tell him I had failed at becoming a mother. That he had married the wrong person—someone who couldn't give him a family. All the crazy bullshit that your mind and heart cloud your better judgment with, if you have a uterus.

My stoic brother stepped up to the plate that night. We drove to the hospital, where he was able to fast-track me past the hours of emergency-room bullshit, and straight up to his obstetrics department. His co-workers were kind, gentle, and swift. An ultrasound was completed, and it was determined there was no heartbeat and a D&C was performed. I was no longer pregnant. Just like that.

When I spoke with Dana, we cried, we talked, and above all wished we were in each other's arms for comfort. The procedure was quiet and prompt. My brother tried his best to console me. But in hindsight, it was hard for him, too. Now that I am older, maybe it was because I was his little sister... Or maybe because he didn't want to show too much emotion around his co-workers. His descriptions and explanations to me were clear and succinct. When I was ready, he drove us back to his house in Canton. I was then scheduled to fly home as quickly as I could.

The following morning, I was numb. Like a slideshow of all of the hopes, plans, and dreams of our marriage and budding little family had been stomped on, shit on, broken, and left to be forgotten. Later that morning, as I was trying to keep myself together for the flight home, my brother spoke briefly about the previous night. I know he tried to help comfort me by giving me information, with lots of details. Although I was not receptive or even cognizant, at the time, the information he provided proved essential to my moving forward, and I am forever grateful.

During the D&C, the doctor performing the procedure noticed an abnormality in my uterus. My clear and concise medical training comes in handy here: my uterus looked more like a heart than a triangle. Meaning that the upper center, where stupid people close their fingers together in

God-awful Instagram posts to show their "love," was where pregnancies would likely attach to my uterus. And although it meant I could very possibly become pregnant again and again, those pregnancies would never remain viable through a full-term pregnancy. If they attached there again, the likelihood of additional miscarriages was quite high. In layman's terms, I had a birth defect in my uterus that could only have been discovered when a miscarriage happened *and* if a caring and attentive doctor noticed. At that time, it sounded like gibberish, and I wasn't prepared to receive it.

But then I was. Back in Colorado, I met with a reproductive specialist. My uterus was repaired surgically. When it was safe and healed, we were able to try to conceive again. And we did.

As luck would have it, I realized I was pregnant after three long, drunken nights in Vegas and a hangover I just couldn't kick. Dana and I walked out of our hotel, Planet Hollywood on the Strip, to the Walgreens down the street, giggling with excitement the whole way there. Not surprisingly, we were the *only* couple in the pregnancy test aisle excited to be there. The others (yes, there were a few) looked like deer in the headlights.

We bought some tests and walked back to our hotel. We had already checked out of our room and had planned on squeezing in as many free drinks at the craps and poker tables as we could before having to leave for the airport. Since I could not wait to know, I took both pregnancy tests in the lobby bathroom of Planet Hollywood, like the classy broad that I am. They were both positive. And we were both certain that we wanted, deserved, and were more than ready to be parents.

A few months later, I was still giddy with pregnancy fever and finally past the three-month mark of feeling like absolute shit, certain I was in the clear, as I drove home from work. By this time, we had bought our first home, a little bungalow that needed a ton of work but had a ton of potential and had cemented our plans to become real-life, responsible, and married adults.

It was rush hour, but I was close to my exit. Just one quick turn and I would be home. The last thing I remember was turning and watching the headlights of a car slam into me, and airbags exploding, instant jolting, and utter fear and dread. I don't know exactly who called the paramedics.

I remember screaming over and over again that I was pregnant and I had just had a miscarriage and surgery. Before I was taken away by the ambulance, I also remember screaming at the other driver that he had killed my baby, as I started to bleed. Completely unfair in hindsight, but completely justified at the time.

The ambulance took me to the ER, at which point I was bleeding, sobbing, and praying this wasn't the end again. It just could not possibly be happening again. And yet, I began preparing myself that, inevitably, it was.

I kept thinking about how perhaps my previous sexual and promiscuous poor decisions must have caused this. That this was my fault. Again. And I dreaded the thought of telling my husband and family that I had lost another baby.

At the ER, ultrasounds were completed, and all of the tests were run. The heartbeat was strong. My placenta was intact. My baby was okay. I was okay. Sort of. I gave birth to my first son on April 8, 2005. The birth was uneventful, relatively easy, and he was completely and totally healthy and perfect.

I absolutely loved being pregnant. I was a lovely pregnant person. I looked as though I had swallowed a watermelon, and that was basically it. Not a medical problem in sight. I know how lucky I was and am, as I have heard and learned over the years how births can be profoundly and meticulously planned, yet can go profoundly wrong. I think it was also, in my heart, because of the profound gratitude I felt, carrying my firstborn son. He was *so* loved, wanted, protected.

I was lucky enough to have a second son almost three years later. They are completely different but love each other so intensely, it makes my heart swell more often than not. They are kind to each other. They have inside jokes. They make my life whole, full of love. I could not be prouder of each of them.

Now, I will not step up on a soapbox, even though I really want to. Everyone has their own beliefs, dreams, hopes and what have you about pregnancy and children. This is only my story of my firstborn son and our pregnancy, after we navigated some miscarriage landmines. Each and every woman has their own path.

It can be full of completely unknown situations, obstacles, feelings, and relationships that we all, as a whole, know absolutely nothing about. Nor should we.

The ever-present empath in me will only say this: You never really know another woman's story about pregnancy and what their journey is or was. Nor should we.

Crime and Punishment

Crime and punishment. Here's my recipe. Take one educated white girl, add some severely mentally ill teenage girls, add some incarcerated violent adolescents, attorneys, judges, prisons, probation and parole officers, overworked and overwhelmed caseworkers, then sprinkle all of these people with the utter frustration, lack of resources, and consistent, overwhelming disgust of an ill-informed public, and you have my employment history after college. It was the perfect recipe for utter despair, meeting my need for a poorly thought-out hope to be a world-saver.

I originally wanted to be just like Jane Pauley, Diane Sawyer, or Katie Couric. I felt a calling to become a journalist. Maybe because I loved to write, but I think it was mainly because I wanted to do something good with my life.

I graduated high school and began to explore where I would eventually land after graduation. I applied to colleges all over the country and luckily was accepted at every college I applied to. I eventually decided that NYU would be the place for me, that it was where I thought I belonged and was thrilled when I was accepted.

I established my class schedule and even secured a dorm near Washington Square Park, right on the campus.

Before I was set to begin college, my mother and I went to visit the campus in person, meet the resident advisor for my dorm, and dip my feet into New York City. We had a great visit together. It was an adventure for just me and my mom, and I absolutely loved our trip together.

Ahead of time, I had imagined in my head that when I saw the school in person, I would feel an instant connection that would affirm my decision to move to New York. It was the opposite for me; I didn't like the experience at all. I returned to Colorado and decided that NYU was not for me. And given my measly academic scholarship, I recognized, if I decided to pursue a degree there, I would end up shouldering well over six figures of student loan debt. Today, I am grateful that I was smart enough at the time to be more financially pragmatic.

I decided to bench my decision to move to New York, in order to avoid that crippling debt for the rest of my life. And how messed up is that? That, at nineteen, I was lucky enough to know what lifelong student loan debt would do to me, and I decided to take another path. I know, if I was writing for a corny, lovey-dovey Hallmark movie, the thought of foregoing attending NYU, where I would *certainly* meet the man of my dreams, should have been a huge mistake and cause tons of regret. But for me, the universe certainly had other plans. Plans that ended up affording me the most incredible life. Isn't life funny like that?

I stayed in Colorado and ended up studying sociology and criminology. At the time, I was working as a legal assistant for several different defense attorneys. I had met one of them while we were guzzling coffee at the coffee shop near our first house. He was a character and became something of a father-figure in my life, as my relationship with my own dad was strained—well, basically non-existent at that time.

Charlie was a larger-than-life personality, a big man who could fill any room with his boisterous laugh and sense of humor. For some reason, in the coffee shop one day, when he mentioned out loud needing legal help, I jumped at the chance and said I would be happy to help him. Of course, I did not know *anything* about the law, how to draft a motion (let alone a legal letter), how to perform legal research, or how to help with bookkeeping and billing. I did, however, know how to type fast. And that ended up helping me get my foot in the door of his one-man law practice.

If I were to say the job was perfect, it would be a lie. Charlie was difficult and sometimes even cruel in the ways spoke to me, especially when he was frustrated. I think he often forgot about my age, my insecurities, and my lack of experience in law or business. But he also had a hugely motivating confidence in my potential, which made the job more exciting and fun.

He would throw me into a law library to find case law for cases when I didn't even know what that meant. He had me develop defense strategies and help with trial exhibits and witness questions, and I met regularly with our clients. To this day, I still am not sure if I was authorized to undertake some of my job responsibilities. But nonetheless, I did my job as best as I could.

Charlie played such a major role in that time of my life, when I desperately wanted to spread my wings and fly away from my parents and my youth as quickly as I could. Although he was the proverbial bull in a china shop at times, he saw value in me. He made me feel strong and smart and capable. He taught me about jazz music, his personal obsession. He introduced me to others as his professional assistant and made me feel less like a kid and more like a responsible, able-bodied adult. Unfortunately, though, there were times when his clients were of questionable character, and I was forced to work with them directly.

Toward the end of my tenure with Charlie, he began to represent mainly men accused of domestic violence. As you can probably imagine (but not to stereotype), these clients were somewhat slick and sleazy. And they really loved that their defense attorney had a young, attractive legal assistant helping him whom they could ogle.

I did have to tell one client that my name was *Erin* and not sweetheart, babe, or gorgeous. That client was accused of stalking and beating his girlfriend, with irrefutable pictures to prove it. Toward the end of my time in that law office, I had an attack of conscience about working with abusers like that, based on my own experiences. It was one thing to represent people who had received a DUI after an evening (or several) of bad choices. But these abusers left me feeling like I needed a shower by the end of the day.

I eventually left my job with Charlie, but it was one of the longest jobs I ever held. I can honestly say that, until working with Charlie, I had never had a job that taught me so much. I learned about human behavior, the law, my relationship with my dad, and my own possibilities and potential. I stayed in contact with Charlie over the years afterward. We would meet for coffee and lunches from time to time. Dana and I even consulted with him for legal advice from time to time, after we became fully-formed adults. I hold a special place in my heart for him.

Several years ago, I was contacted by Charlie's brother, who told me he had passed away. I never asked how he died, though I have my suspicions. He often made bold pronouncements about his physical health, but I knew he was sugar-coating whatever was really going on with him, medically. I sure did love that guy and have kept the letter of recommendation he wrote on my behalf upon my departure from that job. It was the kindest, most generous, and thoughtful letter, reinforcing what I knew to be true about that big lug. He was an enormous man with an enormous heart.

After that, I thought I would end up as some sort of stealthy, rogue, socially conscious saver of the world who had tons of experience under her belt. This is where my own career path began. I didn't have a master's degree, but if you wanted to work with a deviant population as I did, you had to pay your dues and work in direct care or treatment centers, in order to get your foot in that door.

So, that is what I did. I began to work at a locked, high level of care facility for mentally ill and court-ordered adjudicated delinquent teenagers. I was placed in the teenage girls' unit, thinking it must be far easier to work with girls than boys. Again, I assumed wrong. I was thrown to the wolves, mildly trained, but I put on a brave face and played the role of someone who surely knows what they are doing.

It took some time, but eventually I did learn how to work effectively with this challenging group of girls. However, the job took its toll on me. I led group therapy sessions with the girls, which was fascinating, life-altering, and, at times, terrifying. Based only on the date on my birth certificate, I was the alleged grown-up in the room. But these girls were clearly hardened criminals, who had seen a lifetime of pain, sometimes before they were even twelve years old.

Back then, secondary trauma (also known as the residual trauma a treating professional experiences, when it is bounced off the victim onto you) wasn't really discussed or well-known. But goddamn, I felt it all the time, as did my co-workers. I would drive the thirty minutes from the foothills of Colorado to my downtown apartment and almost forget how I got home, still swallowed up by the stories, their behaviors, their needs. It consumed my life, my heart, and my thoughts. But I believed that feeling that way, while working with such emotionally damaged people, was normal and necessary. I now know it was *not* normal, nor was it necessary. It sucked almost every ounce of empathy and care out of me that I could muster.

I won't unload every traumatizing story, only the ones that I allowed to stay with me, after I left that job. At one point, my sons asked me what my "worst cases" were, during my time were there. There are only three that I care to share. Here goes...

The first was only after being there for a few short months. It was my first time experiencing a true lockdown emergency. The bells were ringing out over the loud speaker of the facility, and the radios blared, "*LOCKDOWN. LOCKDOWN. SOUTH WING LOCKDOWN.*"

Not all of the kids were remanded to this facility due to delinquent behavior. Many were placed there by their own families, who could no longer manage their children on their own, or by social services for intense and substantial mental illness. These patients could not be successful with an average therapist; the normal means of treatment and therapy just wouldn't cut the mustard given their levels of need.

This was the first time I ever witnessed someone come so narrowly close to succeeding in suicide. This girl, age fourteen, had taken two pencils and stabbed one in each wrist after buying privileges and telephone time from other girls to provide her some privacy. She also "bought" things from other girls on the unit discretely. Namely, she hoarded her roommate's pills.

Her roommate had mastered the art of hiding her own required medications somewhere in her mouth (or possibly elsewhere), without staff realizing she had been doing so. This fourteen-year-old girl washed those pills down with broken pieces and shards of plastic utensils from the lunchroom. She began violently vomiting blood, sobbing and screaming, and attempting to throw maniacal punches at me like a modern dance student.

After three other staff members and I were able to successfully restrain her, carry her out, and strap her onto a safety table, we called for emergency help. She was eventually taken to the hospital, and I ended my shift by completing my necessary reports and discussions about the incident with the other staff and supervisors that night.

Completely overwhelmed and exhausted, I eventually was able to go home. When I arrived at my apartment, Dana asked me how my day at work went. And I said, "Fine. It was fine." There is no way he could ever comprehend what had happened, since I couldn't myself. Around this time, I decided that the only people I could share my work experiences with were people who worked in similar fields or situations. After all, they really were the only people who could understand how horrifying humanity can be.

The second event occurred not long after the first. The staff from the female unit had the pleasure of welcoming a male resident into the female unit, if space was limited on the various boys' units. Unfortunately, I ended up drawing the short straw that day.

An angry male resident had been transferred to my unit, as he was unable to manage himself after learning about the death of a close family member. In addition to his loss, his correctional commitment (also known as his sentence from the juvenile delinquency court) had been continued longer than he had anticipated, and he was not happy about it.

He was transferred into our unit's safety rooms, because the safety rooms in the boys' units were occupied. These are the padded rooms designed to keep kids safe, both away from others and, hopefully, also safe from themselves. Although those rooms might feel scary and cold to others, with the level of need these kids had, I recognized they were truly a necessary evil.

I had to go and check on him every hour, to be sure he was safe. I also made a safety plan with him for the rest of each day, hoping this would give him something to think about other than hurting himself or anyone else.

As I entered the room, he stared at me blankly. I assumed, based on how he glared at me, he wished he had his own pencils to shove into *my* wrists. Eventually, I squeaked a few words out of him, making a verbal contract with him to remain safe for at least another hour.

And that's how it was done. Each minute, each hour, each day. Little by little, things do have the possibility of improving, and he said he would try. I found a paperback book for him to read plus some paper and crayons to draw, and I impressed upon him how I recognized he was obviously trying hard, despite what was happening to him. I also explained that his efforts really meant something. He just smirked at me, and I locked the door behind me as I left.

I had other duties that day, but I did come back an hour later to check in with him. I peeked in the cell door window and noticed red all over the walls of the room, while he had his back to the door. Our training had always instructed us that, when you enter a resident's room with the intent of leaving safely, not being able to see a resident's face was unsettling and likely unsafe for you.

I called into the room before unlocking the door. If he had chosen to use the crayons I'd given him simply to scribble all over the walls, I told him I would have to remove them from his room. But he sat motionless, so I called in again. He turned slightly toward me, holding the crayons.

Feeling confident that I had made my point, I opened the door and realized what he had been up to for the last hour. He smiled at me, his mouth full of blood and dripping from his lips. He had first attempted to bite off his own tongue but been unsuccessful. Instead, he'd spent his time during that hour biting off the inside tissue of his mouth and spitting the blood and tissue on the walls, so he could "paint" instead of draw.

I mustered up what fake courage I could show, called for assistance, and rapidly told my supervisor that I needed to clean up in the medical office. I went to the office and burst into tears in a closed room. I was terrified and ill-prepared to see that kind of carnage up close and personal.

But, of course, I presented myself as a competent treatment practitioner who could likely handle anything. Nothing could have been further from the truth. For months after that event, I had horrible nightmares. I had to recount what I'd seen repeatedly for administrators of the facility and to the family of that resident.

I now feel I have safely put that experience to bed. However, on occasion, I do still see his face, his mouth, and all the blood. I can only hope he eventually found some sort of peace in his life. But again, it was another devastating look into the inhumanity of humanity. His own family history of abuse, addiction, and poverty was extensive and awful. I truly believe he never had a chance.

The third and final case during that job involved a lovely seventeen-year-old young lady. She was 6'3" and was there purely as an attempt to try to keep her from walking down the street and shooting someone for the sheer joy and thrill of violence. She had no interest in following any rules or in believing she had a chance, either. Bottom line, she was mean and terrifying to the other girls on our unit. And that made her happily sociopathic in nature, almost daily.

Today, I can look back and know for sure that she probably did have a myriad of mental health diagnoses, but she had planted her feet firmly in the ground as a straight-up criminal. And that was why the juvenile court system forced her to be placed in our facility, instead of in jail. This was with the hope that she would one day see the light and use her time in treatment to improve herself. As you can probably guess, that never happened. Her demeanor and attitude could change in a flash, and her hair-trigger volatility kept all of the unit's staff on high alert from the beginning of our shifts to the last minute.

This night was no different regarding her attitude and behaviors. I was leading a creative writing group with the girls, and I had given them each an easy assignment to work on. I cannot remember exactly what the assignment was, but I always tried to keep things simple. The writing assignments were always something that I hoped wouldn't stir up too many things inside of them that could potentially cause trouble.

After the assignment was given, the girls scattered throughout the main commons area to work. I walked around to each girl, making sure they stayed on task and answering any questions I could.

This lovely girl was on one side of the room, while another unlucky girl was on the other. Light music was playing to calm their nerves, and the other girls were talking quietly and writing. Then, as quick as a lightning bolt, the lovely and angry young lady leaped over the couch, pushed me to the ground, and jumped toward the unlucky girl on the other side of the room in a motion I can only describe as a superhero leaping to make a last-minute save. Only she wasn't saving anyone—she wanted to kill someone, or everyone, in the room.

Again, the alarms went off, and my lovely friend was tackled and carried by six staff members to the safe room that had been previously painted in blood.

As expected, she wasn't going down without a fight. My team decided, since I had somehow developed a relationship with this girl during our writing exercise, I should lead the "takedown," where we would have to forcibly enter the room with our safety equipment to restrain her until she could calm herself. Ultimately, our goal was that she not hurt anyone else or herself.

It felt like the police executing a search warrant, and I was the lucky one at the front of the pack. By the time we had gathered double the number of staff to complete the average takedown, based on our experience with this girl's level of aggression and violence. By the time we were prepared to enter the room, she'd had enough time to urinate everywhere plus throw and wipe feces on all floors and surfaces.

I tried to muster courage, and we called out to her to alert her that we were entering the room. She was standing on top of the restraint table, crying, covered in shit and piss, and telling me to fuck off in every possible combination of words. I told myself, she is scared, and this is *all* scary and based purely in fear. But we had a job to do, so I entered the room.

At that moment, one of the staff members behind me said something I couldn't hear or understand, so I turned my head back to look. A split second later, as I looked back at my lovely young lady, she had decided to use the legs on her 6'3" frame to swing a kick at my head with every ounce of her being.

By some miracle, I jolted my head back, and my hair flew in the breeze made by her giant feet and leg. I dropped to the floor as the other staff rushed her, restrained her, and I tried to help. She remained restrained far longer than I had expected. She growled, snarled, and spit at us all.

I pretended like I was okay afterward. I had done the best I could. When I went to be decontaminated by the medical staff, I asked, for the first and only time, if I could go home early. And I quit the next day.

After those experiences, I decided to take it up a notch. Still believing that this kind of employment, doing this type of work, was where I was destined to be, I applied to work in the main juvenile detention facility for our area. My mother had worked there from the day the facility opened and was adored by the staff and the inmates there.

You read that correctly: my sweet, loving, patient, and smart mom worked as a mental health coordinator with kids even more violent than the ones I had just worked with at the treatment center. It was lovely to work with her. The kids (also known as inmates) revered her with such kindness and patience. She had difficulty with poor hearing and the inmate accommodated her, and they loved how she made them feel heard and loved. It always blew me away, seeing these criminals (even though they were kids) treat and talk with my mother with care, empathy, and kindness. At times, I used to wish that those who wished to lock those kids away forever could only see what these kids were capable of. Seeing that firsthand, as her daughter, was something I feel really lucky to have witnessed and been a part of.

I bounced around in different positions there. I spent a great deal of time attending initial hearings for kids after they were first arrested. I was on-call overnight sometimes and would conduct screenings on scene with police officers, after they had arrested kids for various crimes. I would make bond recommendations, propose release conditions, watch kids pee into cups, and place ankle monitors on them. It really was surreal when these seemingly infant children would return home to their frustrated and often devastated parents to wait for their court cases to play out.

Just as with adults, sometimes these kids were violent. In fact, they were often violent. But at least there, unlike at my last job, the support and staff were readily available to help and break up fights and underground plans to riot or stab someone. I never had to put my hands on another child again, thank goodness. But it did always feel as though things could turn violent at any moment.

One day in April 1999, while I was working there, I sat in my office reviewing a court docket and a list of the myriad marijuana-using car thieves I needed to interview for the following day's hearings. I heard what has now become all too familiar. Just like on 9/11, everyone, especially in Colorado, remembers exactly where they were when they heard about the massacre at Columbine High School.

This high school narrowly bordered the jurisdiction of kids held in our facility. We had had high-profile cases in the state in the past. But nothing, of course, like this. As the terrible day unfolded, we were told, if authorities were able to apprehend the shooters from the school alive, the possibility of housing them in our facility was very real, in order to afford law enforcement the space to do what they needed to do in their jurisdiction. As we all well know, though, that was not to be. Those two shooters did not live to be apprehended by the police. But to say that day in April did not profoundly change me, change us, and still affect us to this day, would be a lie.

I learned every little nugget about the juvenile delinquency system in that job. I met with kids incarcerated for everything from truancy to murder. As you can imagine, the latter group has stayed with me like a tattoo.

I had been in my job for some time and eventually graduated into a position of supervising the other case managers in our unit who were also responsible for making initial bond recommendations for each offender. Due to that position, and since a young, fourteen-year-old girl had just been arrested for murdering her mother, yours truly was assigned to meet with her upon her entrance to our facility.

In the great state of Colorado, at the ripe age of fourteen, you can be charged as an adult for capital crimes—like murder. This young lady had shot and killed her mother while living on a horse racing track during the racing circuit season. When she was arrested and admitted, I sat in the holding cell, looking at her. She looked disconnected from reality but seemed at ease as she sat there while I explained to her what would happen in the next few days.

I didn't know the details at the time but would later learn that she had survived endless experiences of torturous sexual abuse by her mother's boyfriend. Her mother had left that man multiple times, but then proceeded to welcome him back into their lives over and over again. They were traveling horse racers and lived in trailers from town to town, never affording this girl any sort of stability in her life in any way.

Her defense attorneys would later argue that, when her mother brought this man back for the last time, the teenager couldn't bear it any longer, and she shot and killed her mother. This was the first time I sat, face to face, with someone who had chosen to kill another person.

For the state to argue that she should be charged as an adult for murder, a transfer hearing needed to be held to determine if the juvenile case should be transferred to the adult criminal system. By the time her transfer hearing was scheduled, she had been a resident in our facility for well over a year. In that time, I was required to meet with her regularly and report back to her defense attorneys regarding her behavior and status on the female unit. As time progressed, she quickly and alarmingly began to regress, becoming more and more childlike and immature every day. When I met with her, she would draw me pictures, skip through the halls, and giggle like a second grader.

I was eventually asked to testify regarding her behavior during her time at our facility and to draft a report for the court to that effect, for her transfer hearing. During one of the last visits that I had with her before her hearing, she and I took a walk through the facility and the courtyard to check in.

Her immaturity was on full display by this point, and it was eerily palpable. She lacked any sort of physical boundaries and would hug me, lean her head on my shoulder, and write notes to me with hearts over my name. Eventually, she told me she wished she could stay with me, so I could act as her "new" mother. The eerie irony of her comments was never lost on me. Yet, my heart broke for her every time we would meet. Truly, that girl never had a chance.

Thankfully, the court felt the same way I did and ended up not sending her down the toilet of the adult penal system. The case was profoundly important to me and taught me so much about the human condition. Could she have been a sociopath? A psychopath? I don't know. But some adults sure do work extra hard to destroy their kids' lives sometimes. This led me to my next and final stop in my treatment/corrections/social work career.

I left the correctional system and stopped working with my mom. It had been an incredible gift; one I know very few will have that opportunity to enjoy. But working there together created such a wonderful, lifelong connection between my mother and me, far beyond just mother and daughter. And yes, my mom was a badass at that job.

If my previous two jobs had not cemented this career path for me, I then decided to become a caseworker with our county social service agency, in order to keep trying to save damaged people who didn't want to be saved.

I used everything I had learned thus far and became an adolescent caseworker. I began to work with a team of some new and some well-seasoned caseworkers. I put everything into my work and jumped in to help save the world again. I had left a jail and now felt like I'd been granted freedom as well. I was surrounded by like-minded people who had twisted senses of humor like mine, and we shared tender hearts, truly wanting to help others.

Our team was a brigade of teenager fixers, and I loved it. It was interesting, draining, and enlightening all at once, and I have since met the world with totally different eyes after working in social work. But as is the case in every emotionally draining job that lacks any possible positive ending or decent paycheck, I couldn't do it forever. I was far too keen to open my heart wide open, in the interest of doing whatever I could to try to do the best job I could. I noticed when I started to dread my job instead of love it. The families I worked with began to harden my heart rather than the opposite, and I realized I couldn't continue down this road for much longer.

In 2005, I gave birth to my first son. Up until then, I was naively chock-full of parenting advice for other parents without being one myself. I mean, how hard can parenting *really* be? I was certain I knew better than anyone. But when I was finally a parent myself, anything and everything began to hit way too close to home. Don't get me wrong: despite my better judgment, the kids that I carried on my caseload often burrowed into my heart. All despite my efforts to keep them at an arm's length, as I was trained to do. I had such difficulty doing that. It is the fatal flaw of the empathetic—welcoming in the unhealthy people for us to fix.

The last case, the one that did me in, was an incredible family, and I still think of them often. I was assigned to work with a teen girl, a sixteen-year-old, strong-willed runaway prostitute. She was brilliant—like savant-level brilliant. She was just stuck in a cycle of bad decisions, bad habits, bad friends, and bad people all around her, except for her single dad, with whom she and her younger sister lived. Her dad, who was her biggest advocate and cheerleader, never gave up on her.

When I first met her, she would regularly fall apart, run away, get arrested, eventually end up back home with some help, and then start the whole cycle all over again. I know the father was frustrated and overwhelmed. And I also know he wasn't too proud to ask for help with his daughter. I always admired his grace in that regard.

The last time she came home, it felt different. Really different, as if she'd finally gotten it and wanted to make some major changes in her life. It was as though it wasn't just her dad and me who wanted more for her; she wanted it for herself, too.

I was so hopeful for her and had made appointments for her for a few weeks later, to apply for a program at a community college part-time and return to high school once and for all. I remember her dad and I giving each other a high-five for successfully crossing the finish line with her, hoping things would all be okay now. But they weren't. A few days later, her "friend" (aka pimp) had apparently contacted her. The allure of her previous life was just too tempting for her to refuse. And she ran away again.

I came back to work that following Monday and listened to her heartbroken dad, who had left me a voicemail, explaining how terrified he was that she had left again. He said he could usually find her in certain places around town, and he would try there again the following evening, if she didn't return home before then. I called him, and we spoke briefly about his daughter. I tried to reassure him that I was certain she would eventually come home again, as she always did, and to not give up hope.

The next day, I called him to see if she had returned, and he didn't answer. I later learned he had been driving all over town, all night long, looking for her. He had returned home, had a massive heart attack, and died. I believe he died not of a heart attack, but of a broken heart. It was too much for me to bear. There was only a small portion of my own heart left after all of these jobs, and I decided it was time for me to leave that job, too.

These jobs were based on my interest in working with those involved in deviancy, crime, and mental illness. But as I look back, the real crime was two-fold. First and foremost, it was always with the kids. I never assumed that every kid I worked with was innocent and didn't bear any responsibility for the choices they had made. They did need to be given appropriate punishments, resources, and treatment.

But the second crime was assuming that those who work with this population are prepared and able to handle it. These people I worked alongside are not willing to discard these kids like garbage, like a lot of people would. They are warriors that aren't paid as such. They walk into work each day with the idea that *today* will be different and special. And, more important, that these people are worth all of it.

All of the misguided reviews, reports, case notes, and ill-advised unwarranted critiques from people who never removed a child from the only home they may have ever known at 4:50 p.m. on a Friday. They are spent people. Spent on the horrors of others' decisions to put themselves and, really, *anything* before their own children.

The expectations for anyone in this kind of work often seemed, and still seems, impossible and unreasonable. The most truthful and honest way to describe those who choose to work in this field, I believe, is to accept that these families *all need help*. But they are rarely willing and accepting of that fact. And it doesn't matter who delivers that message—those families must be able to receive it.

I distinctly remember thinking to myself shortly after I miscarried, before my first son was born, there was an utter and awful irony to my job. I was spending well over forty hours each week trying to convince parents to keep their precious children, to stop jeopardizing their children's lives, and to do what they needed and were legally required to do, in order to keep their children. But they rarely saw it that way. Rather, they saw the opposite. While I was planning and hedging my bets on another pregnancy, willingly wanting an intrusive surgery, I was simultaneously pleading for parents to just *try* to be parents, themselves. It felt like a cruel joke.

I have so much respect for my fellow soldiers in casework. It felt like a club that required admission based upon a willingness to leave your judgments at the door. For if a mistake is made, you are inhumane. But then again, if you do nothing, you are also inhumane. Each day could leave you decimated, with just the remnants of a heart and soul. In my mind, *that* is criminal.

My biggest takeaway from those jobs was about fear. The fear of failing the families I worked with, the kids I worked with, and the people I worked with.

Sometimes, I still feel that fear. And now, I've been working through my fear of writing about my life and any of my own pitfalls. How close I could have been to making one wrong move and winding up with my very own caseworker or probation officer. Now, I feel a fear of losing even more people than I already have, due to my honesty. I fear I will no longer be the person others have always known, because I know that I have changed. I have changed from the person on whom they have always dumped their insecurities, their problems, and their unwanted anxieties, because I was the easy target.

I feel the fear of judgment of others. I feel fear of losing my own status in my little world, my zeitgeist. I am forty-seven and, truthfully, have more fear now than when I was a teenager. Isn't that just insane? People, or more specifically women-wives-mothers, feel the effect of fear in such a deeply profound and layered way, which is so ingrained in us. It is in our DNA. I believe we are all our own worst enemies, in one way or another.

So, press the pause button, recognize your own worth, and appreciate and value that fear. Take a breath and realize you (meaning me) are worthy of this proverbial pause.

I have always laughed away the "jokes" about how I am the flame to every moth with some sort of emotional/relationship/family problem. These problems of others come at me in spades in the strangest of ways. It isn't just me who notices this phenomenon in my life. At times, it feels like there *must* be a hidden camera somewhere, with a cameraperson behind it saying, "*Hmm,* I wonder if she can handle this amount shit." Or the alternative narrative, "No one could manage this level of bullshit, but I think I will call Erin to see if she can..."

This is not my own little "martyr syndrome." It really isn't. I made a deliberate and conscious effort to leave casework (also known as people-helping) behind. That decision was made *long* after my need to help others became interwoven into the tapestry of me.

Therein lies the dilemma. My heart has guided me, and my first inclination is always to try to be kind, to show grace and understanding, and not to judge others. I have witnessed some of the most awful things that humans can do to one another, to their loved ones, to their kin, and their children. I have met murderers for whom I have felt incredible empathy. I have met horrific people who have left me questioning every tenet of my being. I have held children down for hours, as they spit blood, threw their shit on me, screamed, and attempted to end their lives to stop their own pain. I helped a parent desperately try to locate his daughter who'd run away, again, to sell her body, only to see that frantic parent eventually die from a literal broken heart. I helped represent domestic abusers, who had left bruises and injuries on their "loved ones" in a "heated" argument, likely not for the first or last time.

I have seen what humanity sometimes has to offer. And I firmly believe that my tender heart can be a blessing and a curse. I screw up often. I always seem to forget birthdays, phone calls that need to be returned, heated arguments, and things I may have said. Sometimes, I think I have earned a blue ribbon in the "disappointing others" category in the contest of life. But you keep going.

This is why I am still here. Dana and I tell each other often that you just have to get up every day and keep going. I am not saying you forget or change your own core values for other people. I like to think of my core values as the basic menu in a twenty-four-hour diner. You can show up there at 8 a.m., 2 p.m., or 2 a.m., and you will always receive the same food, the same service, and can take comfort in that consistency.

But that does not provide for the need to protect your own heart. What I have learned from my previous jobs and in the process of writing this book, although I have spent many years trying to protect the hearts, minds, families, and feelings of other people, no one will be, or has been, doing the same for me.

I have only myself to blame for not recognizing that sooner. I assume that, right about now, my therapist is looking over her schedule to see how soon she can get me in. Again. But this is the truth I know whole-heartedly about myself. Despite my most egregious faults, I generally find a way to forgive. I forgive most people, so I no longer must carry their shit with me forever. This will also forever be my downfall. It will be my burden to bear, because of my decisions to bear it.

Those are female fears. What about male fears? I have thought about that a lot, of late. I know that fear can appear for men in many different forms. They have inward fears that women can only imagine. They have outward fears that appear on a surface level clear as day.

Machiavelli said, "Men are driven by two principal impulses, either by love or by fear." I never really digested that quote until it was directly in front of my face. My husband and I, as a couple and as the best of friends, have worked through many different forms of this fear. I know he was fearful of me leaving him, and I know he craved indelible love.

And to be truthful, who *doesn't* crave love? In all its forms. When we are at our worst, our lowest, and when we are thoroughly honest with ourselves, it is really what we all fear and what we will forever crave.

Adventures

We all *need* adventures.

I know I loved the crazy adventures I experienced as a younger person, but I truly value the adventures I can continue to have as an adult. I have been blessed with some exquisitely lovely high-end vagabond friends. These are my fellow travelers and friends who, fortunately, know far more than I do when it comes to international travel, luxury, and style. I, however, am a savant at overpacking and lack of planning.

I have a high school buddy, Ashley, who was living in Dubai, and in late 2012, she began to plan a fun girls' trip to Eastern Europe for us the following year. She learned that one of our favorite bands, an epic group from our formative years, Depeche Mode, would be staying in hotels she managed as a PR executive during the Eastern Europe portion of their tour. Ashley thought, what the hell? We should stay there, too!

Never mind the fact that these hotels were epically decadent, the thought of jumping ship from Colorado and heading to Europe sounded like a perfect escape to me. When I opened her random email, I read it aloud to Dana and never expected his response.

He bluntly said, "Just say yes. Go. I want you to go, and you may never have this chance again."

So, before I could second-guess myself, I responded to her email with my excited acceptance and then realized I would have to figure out the details afterward. And luckily, I did. I was able to make the trip happen. Mind you, I was the only one of the group with two small children at home and school responsibilities to organize and manage, but what the hell? Why not? And I had the added bonus of an ample push from my husband.

But I never expected to have the kind of trip we ultimately had.

We coordinated the trip like a shuttle launch, all three of us—one of us living in Dubai, another in Los Angeles, and I was a mom from Denver—were all able to turn our keys at the same time to ensure that this launch was a go. So, just like that, I headed to Eastern Europe as a touring groupie with my two dear friends. A mom of two small boys was running away—it was insane but amazingly fabulous.

I was off via Denver to Minneapolis to Amsterdam, and finally landing in Budapest. I felt a wee bit delirious after a long, long day of travel, but I finally made it to our luxurious hotel.

I was the first of our group to arrive. I tried to take a small nap to ease the jetlag, but to no avail. It was all too exciting for me, and there was no way I was able to sleep. Instead, I went to the hotel lobby, grabbed a glass of wine in the elegant lobby, and people watched while I waited for my friends.

Lo and behold, members of the band and their crew sauntered into the lobby bar as I sat there. I began to look around, wondering if anyone else was seeing what I was seeing? Did they even know how remarkable these gentlemen were? That they would end up in the Rock and Roll Hall of Fame? Regardless, it was the start of an amazing adventure.

My other two friends, Ashley and Paige, eventually arrived at our hotel in Budapest, and we decided upon our plot to be the best American Depeche Mode groupies we could possibly be. In other words, the coolest and least obvious superfans, while maintaining an even cooler demeanor as we stayed in their same hotel. We constantly surveilled the lobby and the hotel restaurants, so we could be sure to join the band for dinner in those same establishments. I was not as well-traveled as my travel partners, but I tried my absolute best not to show my naiveté.

The beautiful hotel where we stayed was gorgeous. Given my friend's job, we were treated quite well indeed. Together, we explored Buda, and we explored Pest. We often looked across the hotel room at one another and giggled about the fact that we had made this trip happen. How, after all these years, were we able to do this?

We stayed in that hotel in Budapest long enough to meet most of the band. We "randomly" bumped into them in the restaurant lobby bar. At random exits of the hotel, we asked one of them for a cigarette. Then, we "randomly" spoke with their publicist about their future eastern European tour dates and how to reach the band and their mates while on the road. Still, all strictly "random."

ERIN HUNT

While in Budapest, we saw their concert and had backstage wristbands that made us all feel like we were eighteen years old. It was magical. We ate sushi at Nobu in the hotel, all while creeping in on the band and their crew in the private dining room. That, of course, was *not* by accident, as we had the luxury of anonymity, excitement, and gumption.

We eventually left Budapest and jumped on a train headed to Vienna. We laughed and reminisced about our high school adventures, while lamenting that we were growing older. But we acknowledged how lovely it was to travel as adults with financial means. When we arrived in Vienna, we headed to another hotel, all care of Ashley's employer. To describe this hotel in one word, it would be *luxurious*. An amazing hotel with courteous staff and exquisite accommodations, to boot. We had a large suite in what I consider to be the most beautiful city I have ever visited.

We were there to celebrate Paige's thirty-eighth birthday. So, that night, we headed out on the town in Wien. We ended at an underground jazz club, which was hidden away and amazing. We toasted to our amazing lives, our long-lasting friendships, and the future. And we sang, laughed, and laughed even more.

The next day, we reached out to the band's publicist, hoping again to "randomly" run into the band at their concert in Vienna. While we couldn't make that happen, she did offer us tickets to the following show, in Bratislava, Slovakia.

146

We didn't have reserved accommodations there, but we made the necessary arrangements and, of course, said yes to the tickets. We decided, instead of driving to Bratislava, we would instead take a river ferry down the Danube from Vienna on the day of the show. The ferry ride was beautiful, passing castles nestled in the forests alongside the river.

When we arrived at the stadium for the concert, it was sold out. The venue was an old, dilapidated soccer stadium covered in graffiti and overflowing with Depeche Mode fans. These were the kind of fans who have photos of the band tattooed all over their bodies, and they were *obsessed*. It ended up being the kind of concert I can only imagine mirrored a sold-out European football game. During the show, we screamed the lyrics to every song. We sang, we drank, we danced, and we hugged each other over and over again. It was a magical night, filled with friendship and memories, and I am forever grateful I was there to experience it.

Later, the night became even better, if that was even possible. We left the stadium after the show and contacted the band's publicist. We ended up meeting them all at their hotel in Bratislava for drinks in the lobby bar. Still high on the energy from the concert, we consorted with the band, their crew, and one another at the bar. We were the silly American girls whom they had just "randomly" met in Hungary. We were the silly American girls sitting on top of the world.

As I mentioned, we did not have accommodations for ourselves in Bratislava, so Ashley arranged for a limousine service to come from our hotel in Vienna to Bratislava and pick us up. And that they did. The hotel sent a decked-out BMW and driver to retrieve us. We said our heartfelt goodbyes to everyone and headed back to Vienna on the Autobahn. We were notably drunk on laughter, drunk on friendship, drunk on memories, and just plain drunk. As we sat in the car, we all sang Michael Jackson songs all the way back to the hotel.

I have explained to my kids how important it was for me to say yes to taking off to Europe with my friends. More importantly, I have explained how I wish very much that they will have the same kind of adventures in their own lives. And the most memorable thing for me, even before I left on this trip, was how their dad told me to say yes to the trip before I could come up with my litany of reasons to say no, instead.

I still try to use that approach to many of my life decisions. As an adult, it is so easy just to say no, without hesitation. You can say no to life, and you can say no to the unexpected. You can always say no to the risky, just because of the risk of being risky. But there is something very liberating about saying yes without thinking. I believe that is when you step off the cliffs of life without looking down first.

It may not always positive and maybe not always is smart; most important, it may not always safe. But man, what if you just sit and simmer in the uncertainty for a while, sit in that uncomfortable feeling, and *then* decide what to do? The rewards feel like your own, not what you "should" always do, but they are *your* rewards. It may not necessarily be safe, but it affords you the possibility of having your own adventure.

I hope my children have their own adventures. Maybe with our little family or with their friends, but most importantly, by themselves. My two cents for other parents living with the constant worry of screwing up their children: *stop*. Spoiler alert: it is highly likely that you probably already have.

If you say yes to your kids when they fully expect you to say no, that moment of revelation, of surprise, will remind them that we all need adventures, and life can be surprising. Even their dear, old, somewhat lame parents can be refreshingly surprising. That, to me, is living the adventure.

Friendships

Let's talk about friendships. Friendships. The old ones, the new ones. What expectations do you have for your friendships?

Everyone talks about how, when a couple divorces, you sometimes end up divorcing some of your friends, too. What about the friendships that feel like family to you, like a chosen family? And what do you do when those close friends, this chosen family, betray you? I used to think it was important to show how strong and resilient I am, despite everything I've ended up learning about friendships with people whom I *thought* I knew. Turns out (spoiler alert), I didn't really know any of those people at all.

I know there are always signs of impending doom in toxic friendships. You can see it coming like a bad car accident, where you freeze in your tracks when you should have run in the opposite direction. In those cases, you can brace yourself for impact. But for me, I didn't see anything coming. I hit the guard rail at eighty miles per hour and went straight over the proverbial cliff. That's the feeling of the sucker punch of learning of betrayals by your own chosen family.

My friendships were integral to my existence. These friendships were with the same people, some for over thirty years. This chosen family was always something I could lean into when I needed them. They were the people who loved my family as their own. We were always together. Every birthday, holiday, parties, card games. The foundation of these friendships, where my investment was and remains, is in loyalty to others. For the most part. I sincerely thought I could rely on and trust these friendships because, after thirty years, who wouldn't?

I was dead wrong.

The little voice in my head over the later years kept telling me that Dana and I were being taken advantage of by some of these friendships. Mainly financially, as our business became more and more successful. It was readily assumed that we would pick up the check at dinner, the tab at the bar, or the responsibilities of helping someone in need, because we could. In the beginning, it gave Dana great pride to show his friends how his hard work was paying off. He has always been one to pay things forward to those around him. Unfortunately, that financial expectation began to rise and rise, until I couldn't sit by and watch it happen anymore. We began to distance ourselves from the obvious culprits and patted ourselves on the back for being so mature.

What I know now about my friendships is that, in many instances, I clearly had much more invested in them than I realized. As I move forward in this new stage of my life, I can look back and recognize those people who did not have my best interests at heart. In fact, they were hedging their bets that our marriage would fail and that my husband would be better off if he left me.

These are people I'd cried with, whom I'd trusted and confided in. It turns out, however, that not all lifelong friendships are meant to be lifelong. Not everyone is supposed to stay. I now think of my life as having been strained through a colander, and those who were supposed to be here still are. The rest had been circling the drain for a long time and just needed to go.

As any good wife would do, I assumed that my stoic nature and aversion to conflict would guide me to a better self in the end. What a crock of shit. You know what feels good? Like, *really* good? Surprising those people who assumed they knew me by screaming at them, cursing them, and telling them to genuinely fuck off. You know what else feels amazing? When you can surprise people with your unwillingness to put up with betrayals anymore. Especially when the expectation was that I would be steamrolled into accepting these betrayals. It turns out life feels pretty great when you take back that control of your friendships. In this new chapter of my life, I am proud of doing that. Doormat no more.

So now, let's talk about *parasites*. I know that sounds bizarre, but I believe I have been surrounded by parasites for quite a while: by beings who feed off your well-being. More specifically, beings who cannot survive without milking you for whatever you possibly have to offer.

It has taken me a very long time to make this connection to my own life. To see that there are those out in the world who utilize others' lives, love, and selves to feed until they are full. You can give to those parasites. Give them what they need at the pace they need it. But they are never really full. They will always want more and continue to take, take, and take.

This unfortunate realization has come at considerable cost. And I don't really know how these parasitical relationships all began. Everyone says certain people are gluttons for punishment, which may very well be true. But what happens when you realize you no longer need that punishment? Or no longer want the punishment anymore?

Look at yourself in the mirror and realize your internal dialogue hasn't changed for a very, very long time. Since you have deliberately sacrificed yourself to people who have willingly gobbled you up, how in the world could you expect anything else to change when you really haven't changed, yourself? I am, in that regard, guilty as charged.

For a long time, I kept thinking that everyone else in the world, everyone within my zeitgeist, everyone I *chose* to surround myself with, needed to change and, apparently, I didn't. What stupid and utter bullshit. The change starts with me and permeates outward, not the other way around. Thinking that others will change before you, yourself, are willing to change is just plain stupid and naive. And to think this truly didn't hit me until I was forty-seven years old is quite telling about who I am and who I was.

The other day, I took a moment—well, several moments, to be honest—to evaluate this realization. How I needed to change my perspective and be whole-heartedly devoted to changing my parasite/host character traits and flaws. Specifically, I admitted there was a flaw to begin with.

I mean, after all, we are all *perfectly* flawed in our own eyes without admitting the need to address our own flaws. Society these days is hell-bent on everyone saying they have problems and the rest of the world should just accept them, to avoid a trigger, avoid trauma, avoid being a victim. But I have a distinct desire to no longer coddle anyone's need to be a victim. It sets a precedent that I deliberately do not want me or my children to adopt. At least not before they examine what part they had to play in each scenario.

Don't get me wrong. I do not say this callously, as though people cannot be victimized through no fault of their own. But the "victim" label is now so far-reaching, I believe it has lost its meaning. Oftentimes, in fact, the common denominators in a lot of poor decisions are the person making the decision, not the person who takes advantage of the bad decision.

I don't know if I developed this mindset because of my self-reliance, my adventurous and independent spirit, my own experiences, or my need to spread my wings far sooner than the experts recommended. But regardless, I am hard-pressed to believe that my kids (or I) will forever be labeled victims of our circumstances, if it happens more than once. Fool me once, shame on me. Fool me over and over again, then it is no longer a mistake and rather a decision I am making and must be held responsible for.

When I decided to undertake this project and try to understand how I got here, I had to take a very long, hard look at my own actions and shortcomings. And I know I have plenty of both. But I also have plenty to offer others in return. I can help and have helped friends and loved ones navigate difficult situations because of my own experiences. That, really, is the true gift of a long life. The ability to provide clarity (when needed), provide empathy (when wanted), and to tap into my own bank of knowledge (when asked).

While that can seem daunting and make me feel *incredibly* old at times, what a true gift it is. Tolerance of poor behavior by you and others leaves no one to blame but yourself. Repeat that to yourself in good and bad times. *DO NOT TOLERATE THE BULLSHIT.*

I have tolerated it for most of my life. I have taken on others' problems under the guise of "helping," but much to the detriment of my own quality of life. This is no longer true for me. I will always be grateful that I figured that part out.

Whenever I looked at others' lives and decisions as "dumpster fires of bullshit," what I was really doing was not allowing myself the grace to observe my very own dumpster fire and learn from it. Instead, I was judging others, so I wouldn't have the space or time to make decisions about my own life, especially whenever my life was a disaster and in shambles. And if *that* is not a self-fulfilling prophecy, I really do not know what is!

Your life is a mess, so mine could not possibly be the same! Alas, bullshit...

Self-righteousness is a symptom of someone being unable to address the undercurrents in their own lives.

After *years* of trying to fix other people, to fix their problems, or fix their children, the time had come for me to fix my own life. And I really think I am on my way there. Not all the way, of course. This "graduate" course in adulting is never-ending.

We learn from our misgivings, we learn from our mistakes, and we learn from our pasts. And I learned, after careful examination, that so much of my life has revolved around "wanters." Those who took and took and took, until I had nothing left, and who then moved on, leaving me feeling empty, as if I had not replenished my own well for their benefit fast enough, and so they went on to the next, to refill *their* tanks instead. And, of course, they left me feeling as though I was to blame.

I cannot stress this enough: I wish I could have figured this out *so much sooner!* But nevertheless, I have figured it out now. Better late than never.

On my list of lifelong wishes for my sons is that they become wise enough to figure out their own balance between being genuine, kind, and caring toward others and knowing when to pound sand and leave. I don't believe there is a manual for that. That there is an understood tolerance threshold for bullshit. I sure as hell hope they both can look in the mirror from time to time and tell themselves enough is enough before too much time passes. Before the shame of allowing themselves to be a "victim" is too profound to admit to anyone, let alone themselves.

I hope they can acknowledge their humanity, in all its vulnerability, as a true gift and not a crutch. And use that humanity to help others. But… I swear to God, if anyone messes with my kids, this Momma Bear will appear with claws and teeth showing, without a second thought. No one will use my sons as hosts to suck the love, kindness, and life from them. They will not fall victim to another parasite. The world is full of hosts, but my kids must *not* be part of that population.

What I also learned was, despite what movies tell you, it really doesn't matter what anyone else thinks. Did it hurt when I learned that friends had lied to me, covered up Dana's affair when he needed them to, and even encouraged him to leave me, to be with this other person? *Of course,* it did! Will I ever trust any of those people again? *Nope.*

The clarity of recognizing truth and lies is devastating and yet liberating, as well. Maybe not at the same time, but both can be true. Scar tissue around my heart is still there. And when it comes to trust, it is still difficult to break through.

One of the biggest takeaways for me is that I never, and I mean *never*, want to be the last in the room to get the joke. Or be the last to know something. That feeling of learning about something everyone else already knows is still difficult to navigate, but not impossible.

I guess the moral of this story is that it might be a *great* idea to shake up your friendships from time to time, to send them through your colander of vulnerability, and then see who circles your drain and who remains. For me, the friends I lost were never really my friends at all. And truthfully, I would argue, they weren't friends with Dana, either.

But even if I had decided to leave him, the friends I have now offer so much support to me every single day, and they never judge me. Those whom I let go of couldn't hold a candle to them. Isn't that some shit?

The Con

I love con artist movies. Second only to serial killer documentaries, they are just fascinating to me. Maybe because of the way certain people can figure out other people's weaknesses, faults, and cracks, can profit from that, getting what they want without their mark even knowing. Or maybe I love the way the culprit identifies and takes advantage of the "tells" of others, deliberately and methodically tunneling into their cracks at unexpected moments.

And there is always the poor sap, the mark, the victim who is oblivious to the cunning moves and deceptions going on, often right in front of their face. When that sap inevitably discovers what everyone else has already known, the humiliation and the anger, the frustration and the hurt boil up and spark in them a need for revenge. The saps will always want their own pound of flesh, their payback, and justice for themselves. In those movies, television shows ,and books, we all cheer on that rightful winner. Justice will have to prevail, correct? And then, it is case closed.

That isn't real life though, is it? Don't get me wrong, I believe karma is real. Its energy is real. It feels palpable, at times. Sometimes, even laughable, like when karma lands in your very own lap. Sometimes, karma feels like the only thing you can wish for, out of desperation or hurt. Like when you may have the best of intentions but still fall short. Even when you may have wished for karma for decades, but it still hasn't graced your life in the ways you desire. And certainly, when you receive karma you didn't see coming. Or worse, maybe—when you deserve it.

I think that is why, with a con, no matter how duplicitous the culprit is and how oblivious the mark, each of them will wish karma on the other. It is a reciprocal relationship, really; like a tennis match that can last an hour, a day, a week, a year, or even decades. I think we all tell ourselves the con from when we are pretty young: that adults have it all together and all figured out. The con is that we adults should not have any faults or flaws. And the biggest part of that con or, rather, lie is that we assume the same about everyone else around us.

I firmly believe that parenting is one of the biggest cons of all. I fully realized this when my oldest child began elementary school. We had decided to move from our home into our current house. My oldest son was finishing kindergarten in a private school, and after we moved, he began first grade at an elementary school near our new home.

Although he was only in first grade, it was crystal clear that most of the parents at his new elementary school had established previous relationships and friendships. It was also clear how I didn't have that benefit, coming from a different neighborhood.

No one warns you that adults revert back to middle and high school-like behaviors when they become parents themselves. It is a phenomenon, a parenting competition, make no mistake. It felt isolating and weird to me.

I have an introverted personality that loves to retreat from other adults, and this made making friendships and relationships with these new parents incredibly difficult and uncomfortable for me, at first. As a family, we also hadn't made any substantial new friend connections yet in our new community, which added to my discomfort.

When I arrived for my son's first day of first grade, I watched the other parents laugh, chat, and point at the people who must be new, because they didn't recognize them. And they didn't recognize me. While you speak to your child out of one side of your mouth, encouraging them to be themselves, to be brave, and to make new friends, secretly you are really saying that to yourself.

I figured these other parents must know what they are doing. Their confidence couldn't possibly be a facade. They couldn't possibly be feeling the same way as me, at the same pace as me. I felt like a flawed and ill-prepared parent who would forever be playing catch-up with those who surely weren't flawed and as ill-prepared as I. Again, that bullshit is a con.

So, I thought the best way to "get involved" was to become a room mom. You know, the mom who shows everyone else how things are done. But I should have done a little research on that first! The truth was:

You are going to rue the day you thought this would be a good idea. You fucking idiot.

My son's first-grade teacher was a duplicitous, mean-spirited woman who should have retired fifteen years before she actually did. She was viciously blunt and cruel under the guise of teaching kids in the exact same way, every year, for decades. She never changed her curriculum, her format, or her awful tone toward the kids in her classroom. And she never, ever changed her expectations of her students or their parents. I thought, as the stupid mark I was, since no one had signed up to be the room mom, stepping in would catapult me into the stratosphere of excellent parents. Again, the joke was on me, only I never saw that punchline coming.

My son's school had elaborate Halloween celebrations every year. These were always preceded by endless meetings with other perfect parents/room moms from the other classrooms, where they explained how they had been working on their Pinterest boards to hand-make gelatin skeleton hands, painstaking activities for six- and seven-year-olds, all while ensuring that peanuts, gluten, offensive imagery, or any other nauseatingly miniscule item that might cause even the smallest amount of discomfort, was avoided at all costs.

The other mothers from the classrooms were granted wide latitude to plan their own parties and activities. I had assumed I would be afforded that same luxury. I would be able to start my very own Pinterest board (what the hell was Pinterest, anyway?) and soon would take the gold medal in parenting with this fucking party. Wrong!

My son's Cruella de Ville of a teacher firmly told me, in words I can only describe as frighteningly blunt and specific, that *her* Halloween party would be *her* way. Period. And it was, of course, as it had been every year prior to my son starting at this school. And more importantly, she said, why would I think about doing anything other than what Cruella wanted and demanded? Sigh. I should have said no. I should have said what I was really thinking. Instead, I dodged her first-grade landmines until my son stepped on one, full force, one day. It was elementary wartime combat, and my son and I were the casualties.

I had been contacted by the school's front office, telling me my son had been called down and held in the principal's office because of an "incident." These was the most frustrating and annoying calls, because they were always stupidly vague and would later prove to be completely unnecessary, I thought. What was especially frustrating was that this school had called more than once in the past for seemingly minor, ridiculous reasons. However, this time proved to be a doozy.

I arrived at the school to find my son sitting in the main office, looking like he had just violated his parole. I spoke with the office staff, who clearly held on to their jobs just because they got their summers off. They seemed to have a poorly veiled need for their own ego-boosting control over kids and parents. And they'd chosen a job where they were surrounded by children—it wasn't as though they were air traffic controllers, holding people's lives in their ill-equipped hands. But what the hell do I know?

Anyway, I signed out my little inmate, who looked at me with his big brown eyes but was unable to speak. I was met head-on by my son's teacher, as we tried to leave the office and get to my car: my own first-grade nemesis.

Veins were popping in her forehead, her arms were crossed across her chest, and she was clearly salivating at the prospect of telling me exactly what my son had done wrong. I took the bait and asked what he had done. She said, as the class prepared each of their items for show-and-tell earlier that day, she had been told by another student that my son had brought a knife into the school. The school district had a zero-tolerance policy with regards to weapons, and my son, my little first grader, needed to be expelled immediately. But, purely due to her saint-like grace, she would not request his expulsion.

That was *her* explanation. The actual explanation was that my son, who had just finished a successful, memorable, and wonderful fishing trip with his dad, grabbed a Leatherman he had used during his fishing trip to cut the fishing line (as well as the other myriad tools included in said Leatherman) on his way through the garage and had placed it into his backpack, as we jumped into my car and drove to school that day.

Standing in the school's front office in front of my son's self-righteousness teacher, I held his hand while tears streamed down his face. I looked into his giant, tear-filled eyes, and my momma-bear rage boiled up inside of me. In the back of my mind, the horror stories about this teacher, her temper, and her inability to show tenderness or kindness only reinforced why I said exactly what I said next.

I held my son's hand hard, and I turned to her and said, "My son is six years old. He is *six. Years. Old.* What in the hell is wrong with you? Do you really think my son brought a fishing Leatherman to school so he could hurt someone? Did you even bother to ask him *why* he chose that item for show-and-tell? I am assuming not. I can, however, assume you believe yourself to know everything about everything. What a great thing that gift must be for you! But make no mistake, if you *ever* speak to my son like this again or place your hands on my child again, I will contact my old work buddies at social services, and we can revisit your incredible teaching practices with law enforcement present."

Recently, I asked my son if he remembered that encounter in the office of the school, and thankfully he said he didn't. But I do. I remember every word, and I remember his big, sad, tear-filled eyes looking at me as though his footing wasn't steady. But he knew his mom would never, ever allow this grown-up to terrorize him ever again.

Long afterward, I learned about this woman's history of physically abusing children in her classroom during her far-too-long educational career. The only person who had been at their elementary school as long as she had was the principal. My son and I have decided that this principal must be an embalmed zombie, because she continued to work there for many years afterward. But my biggest concern was that she allowed this teacher's cruel behavior to continue under her watch.

I was conned into thinking that a good mom follows the expected outcomes defined by their children's teachers and by other parents you may not even know. While I believe this could be true to a certain extent, no one will ever be a bigger cheerleader for your own child than you are. It can prove difficult, though, and you will eat pieces of humble pie from time to time, when your perfect little blessing shows their own humanity or faults or makes mistakes (God forbid). I only wish someone had told me all of this before I stood in that school office, worrying whether my six-year-old son really could be a budding criminal, as his teacher was so freely suggesting.

By that time, I had spent months dropping my son off and picking him up from school. I often lamented my position as the room parent, making me the sacrificial lamb to Hannibal Lecter, my son's first grade teacher. I waited outside the school with the other parents like cattle, all of us pretending we didn't see need to speak to one another. It was ridiculous. My husband was working, so my only respite was after I dropped my little miracle of life, my blessing, my brilliant and perfect child off to school in the mornings, I had some luxurious time to work out at the gym.

Normally, I kept my head down there, listening to my music and building my perfect body, one workout at a time. After time passed, I started to recognize more and more parents from my son's school there, but, shy, I never introduced myself.

One afternoon, while I was waiting for my son to come out of school, two women I saw daily at the gym and the school came by and said hello, suggesting I should work out with them sometime, since we see one another there daily anyway.

It felt like high school all over again. The cool parents had picked me! They knew who I was and had even talked to me...

Where did this whole bullshit idea begin, that the approval of complete strangers is so important? Was it in high school? Middle school? Elementary school? Birth? This never-ending con is real, and I wish I had learned much sooner that I didn't have to be the sucker, the mark, the dummy.

Each year, as my oldest son passed another grade, I attracted, fostered, and cultivated new parental friendships, ones I now carry within my heart and soul each and every day. I know this happened because I allowed these wonderful people into my life and put my false expectations to bed. Rest in peace, old ego and fear and that original con.

I wish, when my kids began school, in addition to each teacher's and grade's ridiculous lists of required items, supplies, and expectations, the school had provided us a list of expectations and supplies for what the *parents* would need, as well. Since they never do, here goes mine!

Kindergarten and first grade: Put yourself out there, and meet new people. They will be your safety net. For yourself and, most importantly, for your kid. If you are lucky, they may become a safety net for life.

Second and third grade: Volunteer to do what *you* are comfortable with, if you can. And if you can't, do not let the backhanded comments, endless emails, and unnecessary requests for more than you can do detract from what you ultimately are there to do: raise a good human who is not an asshole.

Fourth and fifth grade: Let your kid guide the way. If they are unhappy, listen to their reasons why, not to the school's deafening complaints. (This may be geared more toward moms of boys, but that is my wheelhouse.) The complaints may come fast and furious. Or maybe they will never come at all. But as the Boy Scouts say, always be prepared.

Resign as Peacekeeping Envoy!

How do you move on from being a peacekeeper? Better yet, how do you help yourself stop being the designated arbiter of peace seemingly all the time? While maintaining peace attributes to you some lofty qualities you may feel you didn't have before, I don't believe that inserting yourself as the designated envoy into every one of life's peacekeeping missions is really necessary. And here is why.

Peacekeepers look for an obvious middle ground, one where peace between people or positions or sides can be found, sometimes easily and sometimes not. They look for a common subject or feeling about something that two parties can agree on with little to no conflict between them. I think that is admirable. I do. And it is an admirable approach to conflictual situations.

But for me, I have decided that I must sometimes set aside my natural desire to be the designated peacekeeper. Sometimes, I have to step back because of my mood. Other times, it is because I developed a deep disdain for someone arriving late to the party, bent on derailing my NATO-like peacekeeping mission.

For a long time, I let my obsession with keeping the peace overshadow whatever else needed to be said or done. My desire to avoid conflict at all costs was more

169

important than speaking out truthfully about how I felt in any given moment, in order to avoid hurting egos, hurting feelings, hurting friendships, etc. After taking some time to examine situations in my life where I'd stuffed my feelings and opinions away so as not to hurt someone else, I discovered that all those feelings ended up bubbling up in other ways or at times that were, let's say, not ideal!

I'll tell you about one of those situations, though I would be remiss not to add that this was hardly the only time.

I now know that the longer I push these reactions in and down, deep into my gut, the more they will eventually explode in some very embarrassing ways at wildly inopportune moments. I am not proud (well, maybe a *little* bit proud) that yours truly, the lovely woman I like to think of myself as being, would ever completely lose her cool around total strangers, and in public no less. Luckily, I narrowly avoided legal intervention, so chalk up a win for my obvious and observed White privilege. Here we go...

The most noteworthy time I care to share was after I had discovered what my husband had been up to. I had finished yet another obscenely difficult workout at the gym, eaten basically nothing, and was hangry as hell. It was around the holidays, so what better time to visit our local Costco aka walking nightmare?

I was there with another thousand of my newest "friends" from Denver, all of us pining for cheaper toilet paper and paper towels—out of necessity, of course. I beelined through the store, attempting as best I could to grab my "essentials" from the aisles in record time, and then I headed to the checkout desks, where the twenty-plus lanes were simply not enough to handle the holiday volume, each shopper no doubt on the same mission as I was.

I was annoyed. Like, *super*-annoyed. Every time I turned around, someone was in my way, as if they were visiting Ikea for the first time and didn't understand how the carts worked. I "kind of" tried my best to keep my wits about me, but every ounce of me wanted to get the hell out of there and go eat my chips in my car from their enormous bag like everyone else, not spending another second in that crowded, crazy store.

I arbitrarily chose a line and waited. Shortly after I arrived in line, an elderly woman walked up behind me with maybe five total items in her basket. She seemed frazzled by the frenetic energy of the Costco, along with the sheer number of people around us.

As we waited, I kept glancing back at her, thinking how much she reminded me of my grandmother and even my own mother. So, as we crept closer to the checkout, I turned around and said she could go ahead of me. After all, she had five measly items, and I had an overflowing cart and a half, full of stuff for my children who never seemed to stop eating. She thanked me profusely, wished me happy holidays, and walked ahead of me.

Behind this sweet woman was another woman. Not so sweet and gentile. Not so old, and not interested in others. She was talking on her phone, which was on speaker phone for all to hear. A repugnant though benign conversation that everyone around her was forced to listen to, against our will. I heard her yell into her phone that "some woman" let "an old lady" cut ahead of her. This woman then looked at me and laughed, saying, "Well, can I go ahead of you, too?"

I don't know if it was my almost cannibalistic hunger, my frustration with the surroundings, my bubbling annoyance at my own personal marital situation, or just because she happened to be the unlucky recipient of my uncontrollable wrath. But what followed was a switch flipping inside of me, and *I lost. My. Shit.*

Without thinking, I turned around to this awful woman, and said, "No. No, you may *not* go before me."

She scoffed at me, while *still* speaking to some poor person on speakerphone. I heard her say to the unlucky sap that some "dumb woman just let someone get ahead of her" but had not proffered her the same gift.

At that moment, I realized she did not deserve my inborn peacekeeping tendencies, which I normally applied. This mundane situation rapidly turned me into an instigator, a *violator* of peace, and I didn't even care. What followed was not something I am necessarily proud of, but it's a reaction I will not now or ever apologize for, as this awful human needed to hear what I was dishing out to her.

I turned back around and said loudly to her, "Why do you deserve to go ahead of me? What makes you and your dumb toilet paper more important than my things and what everyone else here is trying to buy?" Or something to that effect. And *right* about then, my train went completely off the tracks.

I continued, demanding, "What makes you so damn special? More special than *all* of us around you? Is your stupid shit in your cart any more important than my stupid shit? No, no it isn't. And no one gives a shit about your stupid conversation, either, or you, for that matter."

I turned back around to the sweet old woman I had allowed ahead of me and saw the utter horror on her face. Just then, I realized I had, perhaps, taken this situation way too far. Then I thought, *what the hell? Might as well go down in flames...*

I continued to heckle this woman. I told her in every way possible, as I was quickly checked out by the Costco folks, what I really thought of her and people like her. And it felt amazing. It felt as though all the sugar-coated niceness, the glossed-over feelings, my incessant need for recent years to keep peace no matter was all flushed down the toilet in that moment, and the real me had stepped up to the plate. And I do not regret one word I said to her. Although I am sure, somewhere, there is a random video named "Crazy woman loses it at Costco." Still, it felt so good to be me.

The following didn't feel so great, however. I hadn't really noticed, but a manager had come to "help" me box up my purchases. While this isn't newsworthy, the manager also walked with me through the exit, let me skip showing anyone my receipt, and accompanied me to my car, under the guise of "helping me" load up my groceries.

As we walked, I apologized to him profusely, but also mentioned repeatedly that I was so tired of people treating other people badly and I had just had enough. Not me, of course; just *other* people's behavior. He nervously wished me "Happy Holidays!" and shuffled back into the store.

I sat in my car for a few minutes, trying to compose myself. Then, I proceeded to call Dana, to tell him about what had just happened. I bluntly asked him if he had ever had a manager help him to his car after making a large purchase at Costco.

He quickly said, "No. Never."

I took a deep breath and then said, "I think I was just kicked out of Costco. I should probably never come back here." I began to laugh hysterically. So much for my peacekeeping mission.

I didn't return to that store for a good nine months after that. But it turns out, being an instigator instead of a peacekeeper feels pretty fucking awesome sometimes, too.

Health

Health comes in all forms: emotional, physical, mental, and spiritual. I always assumed that, after my years of intensive workouts, supplements, and conscientious eating, my physical health would come back to me in spades. And it did.

My body was my whole focus for a long time, though not an obsessive way, at least not until the past several years. I followed Instagram accounts about healthy eating, made Mason jar salad dressing recipes, avoided dairy and nuts, gluten and sugar, resisted missing any meals or eating too many meals, enlisted a FODMAP diet, tried keto, tried vegan eating, tried being a pescatarian, tried being a vegetarian, tried celery juice, tried intermittent fasting… I just tried, tried, and tried everything.

I worked very hard to keep in shape, to stop time from affecting my body, and it worked. Almost every ounce of attention I had was laser-focused on my body and how it looked and felt. I fell into the trap of supplement living, plus I started to make cooking reels and videos for other people to watch and "learn." I was all-in for the healthy, stay-at-home mom lifestyle that seemed so prevalent around me.

I even started to make some money from it. I could, if I ever actually did, eat anything I wanted. And if I felt like crap afterward, I knew one of the myriad dieting programs and mentalities would rescue me quickly. Any physical progress I had already achieved would come right back, if I returned to my dieting life of restriction. I safety planned every ounce of my body and ended up decimating it, instead.

It started with a little spot on my leg. It was like a raw, irritated rash that seemed to come out of nowhere. I tried to care for it myself. But the spot eventually grew, and then there were more and more "spots" over my body. It didn't make any sense to me.

I began to see only the spots every day and nothing else. The patches of unhealthy skin became bigger and bigger. I eventually saw my doctor, to see if they could offer me a solution. I started with ointments. And more ointments. And more ointments more often in different combinations. But it kept spreading all over my entire body, and I couldn't hide it anymore. I couldn't hide it from people in public, and I certainly couldn't hide it from myself or my family.

Eventually, I was formally diagnosed with severe psoriasis, along with other autoimmune deficiencies that eventually needed to be diagnosed and treated. Then, I began light therapy at my dermatologist's office, which, for those who aren't familiar, is basically a standing light booth/tanning booth. I started with thirty-second treatments, three times a week.

In the afternoons, I drove to my doctor's office, where I undressed and stood in this strange booth for thirty seconds, wearing goggles. Then, I got dressed and drove home. While the treatments began for thirty seconds each, the whole practice and ritual of going required about thirty minutes each time, from start to finish. It always felt like such a waste of time, but I was desperate for relief.

For well over a year, thinking obsessively about my issues basically became my entire life's focus I even called the light booth "my boyfriend" and named him Joel. My symptoms would mildly subside for a short while, but then, every time, they came back exponentially worse afterward.

And then… 2020 happened. That stupid, damn virus happened, and I was stuck at home with no Joel. I had to go to Plan B. We spent thousands of dollars and purchased my own light therapy booth for my home. I had to cheat on Joel for over a year. But it helped my psoriatic symptoms subside somewhat. Unfortunately, they really were just bubbling under the surface. My autoimmune response to almost anything felt immediate.

In January 2021, I ended up with the Omicron variant of Covid It wasn't fun, as we all know. I had received both of my initial vaccinations but had a terrible reaction to the second one. Should I ever test positive, I'd anticipated my body would react in a profound way.

Having Covid was a perfect storm of terrible factors at war within my body. In addition to my own inability to manage my internal struggles and stress, my body reacted in a way it never had before. My body and immune system felt as though they had exploded from the inside out due to this new and foreign virus. Within seven to ten days of getting sick, my psoriasis covered over seventy-five percent of my body, including my face, my scalp, and my digestive system, my eyes, the inside of my mouth, and the bottoms of my feet. My fingernails started to come apart and fall off. I felt like a leper, inside and out. It was embarrassing and terribly uncomfortable.

Every day, I had to undertake a two-hour process involving creams, ointments, scalp treatments, and long soaking baths in anything I thought would help. I changed my diet. Again. I tried to sleep more, to help me heal, but my body would wake me up and force me to shift around in bed. My body developed internal chills, even while I slept, and those would wake me, too. My scalp began to bleed at night; I would find blood-covered pillowcases in the morning. When the inside of my mouth became almost unbearable, I would vomit after trying to eat and when I woke up in the morning.

After months of staying inside my home like a recluse, too embarrassed to leave, I decided I had to take a different path. I began to feel like this situation and my conditions would never end. During almost three years of increasingly bad symptoms, people stared at me as if I had some sort of condition that might be contagious, especially after Covid began, so I was forced to cover every inch of my body, even in the dead of summer. I finally ended up purchasing Hollywood-level concealer for my face, trying to conceal my sores. Of course, I ended up looking worse.

And the pain—*fuck*. The pain was awful. Each bite of food I wanted to give right back to the porcelain gods. My troubles with eating eerily mirrored an eating disorder, but it wasn't. I *wanted* to eat like I'd used to. I loved to cook for myself and my family. But by the time 3:30 or 4:00 in the afternoon came around, I was always terribly nauseous. I still cooked for my family and tried to remain stoic and strong, but my nausea made cooking very hard. I ended up losing over twenty-five pounds in just a few months, which, frankly, I really did not need to lose. I appeared frail and gaunt; Dana worried I would wither away.

To anybody who asked me about my scars, sores, and plaques, I tried to hide them as best as I could. But my fingernails were falling off, my hair was falling out, and my ability to parent was barely there anymore. My kids grew distant from me, becoming unsure which Mom they would get each day—the one who needed endless hours of sleep, or the depressed, frustrated, and angry mom who felt constantly sick and uncomfortable. Neither option was a very fun person to be around, as I am sure they would tell you today.

I eventually had to beg my doctors to really help me. To really listen to me and not just offer the required protocols. For over three years, whatever they had thought would help me obviously had not worked. I felt like my symptoms and concerns just fell by the wayside, and I was perceived as someone who could not seem to get a grip. They always circled back to the "process" my condition dictated under normal circumstances, which was not well-tailored either to me or to what was really going on.

One weekend, my husband took my children up to our mountain house to ski. At this point, I was avoiding everything and anything that could potentially cause me to become any worse. Extreme cold and the extreme Colorado dryness were not my friends, so I wasn't able to join them.

When he left for the weekend, I'd intended to rest the entire time they were gone. A few days before they left for their ski trip, I'd gone to my local nail salon, where I was a frequent customer, because my fingernails kept falling off. The sweet nail technicians showed me so much kindness every time I saw them. They made special accommodations for me, though I kept ending up with infections or irritations.

During that visit, however, a less kind customer was seated directly next to me. This gem of a human being proceeded to stare at me, glowering with malice, for the entire time she was at the salon, seated next to me. I could tell she was dying to give me her opinion about my physical state but tried to keep it to herself.

Unfortunately, she couldn't manage to do so before I got up to leave. She blurted out to me, "If you have some sort of serious condition or problem, why would you leave the house and put other people at risk?"

Tears flooded down my face, and I told her what I thought she could do with her "concerns," making an uncomfortable scene. Crestfallen, I paid and left the nail salon, feeling like I had a target on my back. My husband left for the mountains the following day, and I didn't even let him know how humiliating that experience had been for me. But by that Saturday night, I had come face-to-face with the darkest place I had ever been.

I woke up in the morning and felt defeated again. I closed my eyes and wished they would never open again. I could not live like this anymore. I had to move every few minutes, as my skin crawled, my eyes crawled, even the inside of my mouth crawled. I felt floods of heat and cold, blood rushes, pumping through my body as I tried to sleep. Nothing had worked, and nothing was helping. I felt I was a burden to my family. I didn't think things would ever improve, so why go on?

Being sick was all I could think about, and I'd started to forget things I needed to do with my kids or my husband, my appointments and responsibilities. Right then and there, I wished for death. I knew it would be horrible for those I left behind, but I didn't see any other way. Anything would be better than what I was dealing with at that time.

I prayed I would die in my sleep. This was the scariest and worst feeling of my entire life. Those wild and pervasively dark thoughts while I was all alone scared the living shit out of me. I am a mother, and my kids need me. I am a wife, and my spouse needs me. I am a friend, and my friends need me. I am a daughter, and my mom and dad and brother need me. If I was gone, what would that do to everyone else?

I sat up in my bed at 4 a.m., went into my bathroom, and stared at my naked body in the mirror. I stared and stared, and then I vomited. I felt as though I would forever appear grotesque to anyone around me. More important, inside, I felt even worse than grotesque.

Large scales of my skin flaked off my body if I merely breathed or moved, and my bleeding sores wouldn't stop oozing. I screamed at my reflection and began to slap myself in my face. I told myself to just die and get it over with. I yelled at myself that I deserved everything I got. I had created this by destroying myself, little by little.

I'd destroyed myself, until my body eventually responded and said, "Your crazy head and emotions have won. Well done, you stupid bitch. You have finally destroyed everything about yourself."

I thought to myself how everyone else had won, too. The world has finally taken its last blow at me, and I'd lost big time. Thankfully, at the time, I hadn't made any sort of concrete plan as to how I would end my life. But I stayed awake until 5:00 in the morning, thinking about how I could do it the "right" way, completely terrified. I finally fell into the deepest sleep out of the pure exhaustion saturating every cell of my body.

I finally woke up late that following Sunday morning, and I had thoroughly scared myself straight. If things had become any worse than they were that night, I believe I would have tried to end everything, end my life, and end my suffering. Thank God, I didn't.

What I did do that Sunday morning was take a long, hard look in the mirror again. I said to myself that I was going to do whatever I could, in whatever way that I could, and at whatever cost, because I *had* to get better. I felt a pull to not end it all, but rather to live for it all. I had been through other tough situations, so how could my body fail me like this? I needed to figure out why.

I refused to accept that this was as good as things were going to be for me. I refused to accept that this was what my life would be like from here on out. I stupidly decided to earn my very own Google M.D. degree. I needed to really understand what having autoimmune disorders meant.

I constructed a timeline to figure out where and when everything in my body had started to rapidly deteriorate. And I realized this was likely my special parting gift from Omicron. I tried to explain my theory over and over to my doctors, but they did not seem to believe me. To this day, I believe it was the culprit, the thing that sparked the internal implosion of my immune system, which ended up fueling my external explosion that had become so obvious to other people. My body, which had already been at a tipping point by that time, wary of anything foreign or stressful, was hit with a foreign virus the equivalent of a 747 airplane. The whole world had never experienced anything like this, not just me. Consequently, we all reacted rather badly, it is safe to say.

I became quite vocal about my condition, and I refused to accept that this was it, that this would be my reality for the rest of my life. In the past, my life revolved had around my obsessions with different diets and medical ointments, along my inability to do some of the most basic of things in life, which I had always been able to do before. I started to see a therapist who helped me to turn a corner. She helped me recognize the deep-seated damage that happened to my body over the course of the past several years. I felt immediately lighter, happier, and more decisive about my decision to dedicate myself to healing.

I must preface this next story with my sincere and most humble confession. I know I am lucky. I know this, I appreciate this, and I fully subscribe to this. I am part of the lucky few who can afford high-cost medications, if need be. So, I finally pulled the trigger and began to pay for biologic injections, to heal my body from the inside out.

When I first investigated this as a possible therapy, I was told it would cost around $9,000 per month for at least two years. Then, the cost whittled down to a modest $500 per month, instead. At that point, I was ready to sell a kidney, sell my home, sell just about anything to get started on a medication that would actually work.

I walked into that next appointment with my doctor on a mission to do something, anything, differently than in the years prior. I wanted my life back and needed it back desperately. Dressed in my hospital gown, it took me a total of maybe five minutes before I began to cry to my doctor. I explained why I was back yet again. I explained that nothing had worked so far, that was clear. And I pleaded with my doctor to help me, that I could not go on living this way.

I did not admit to him that I had just contemplated ending my life. But in my mind, I still had the looping thought that, if he did not agree to prescribe the most intensive protocol of medication and biologic injections, I probably couldn't go on.

He took one look at me and my body and said it was more than clear, my case was very extreme and obviously painful. I felt a giant sigh and release of tension within me. Not just because he was willing to prescribe me what I knew I needed, but that *finally* someone was listening to me and willing to do whatever I needed to get me some sort of relief.

The change in my body was almost immediate. My skin no longer felt like it was melting off me. The awful feeling in my skin, which I so often wanted to scrape away with a razor blade so I might possibly live without so much pain, started to dissipate. And I finally started to feel my body healing. More important, I realized that I could heal my body. If I advocated for myself and demanded that the doctors involved in my care help me in the way I needed to be helped, things could improve.

It didn't take long, and I will continue to use the injections for at least another year, possibly longer. The thought of doing this process for that long is daunting, but I am alive. I am no longer afraid to leave my home. People no longer stare at me or say cruel and insensitive things to me. And now, being on the other side of the worst, feels amazing.

The level of empathy I hold in my heart for people dealing with these types of disorders, especially other autoimmune disorders not physically visible to others, is palpable. The insanity you feel when you know your body is fighting against you, despite your best efforts, is beyond frustrating. It really can be decimating.

Make no mistake, these medications are not a miracle cure. The side effects are awful and last for weeks afterward. In fact, the side effects oftentimes subside just days before the next round starts. It feels cruel to offer your body some real relief for only a few days, knowing it will not last long. But I hope someday to use this pain and my horrible experience in a better way. Each time I give myself an injection, I hear an old-timey cash register ding. I am so very lucky that I can do this every month. How many people out there live with this level of discomfort and pain with no relief in sight? It just isn't right.

Today, I can finally focus on other healing. Healing my body was just the beginning. Healing my heart and healing myself in other ways is a long-term goal for me. I think it just takes a small taste of feeling better in all ways to kick-start everything else.

I am now more in tune with what happens in my body during moments of stress. For me, my biggest health remedy is not just the injections, it isn't going vegan or gluten-free; it is not substituting protein shakes to suppress your desire for a piece of pizza, and it definitely is not pretending that I am okay when I am not. Giving yourself the grace to fail, the grace to appreciate your own pain, and the grace to admit your own mistakes is essential. If given the opportunity, I would prescribe a whole lot of grace to anyone who has made monstrous mistakes or is dealing with pain that just feels unbearable, whether in your heart, soul, or physical body.

Every human being deserves a nudge toward empathy and understanding. This life is hard enough. A pile-on to someone struggling is the most excruciating kind of a health remedy. Before you know it, the things that caused you pain will eventually no longer need a remedy. You will have developed it yourself, with little to no effort. When that happens, it feels fucking great.

Then there is the bigger idea of "health." Once you turn inward and begin to heal your body, you can peel back the layers and heal what's underneath. You can heal the sores that never would heal before. Those sores that creep into your system and steal your health by making you doubt yourself, the ones that fester around your heart, your shortcomings, your insecurities, and your self-doubt.

The funny thing about those sores is that when you heal the first one, the others seem to heal organically, because you are in tune with your own deficiencies. You can recognize where and how you poured your soul into something or someone or anything other than yourself and were left unsatisfied and emaciated.

What I have now learned is that, when you either deliberately or instinctually substitute your own desires and values for something else or for others, you widen your sores inside. The festering becomes exponentially worse. Your "sores" feed off that lack of self-awareness. It is a slippery slope that starts to create a different version of you. A version that, unless you are aware, becomes the newer, "better" version of you. But still becomes unrecognizable.

Health is a twisted thing. Some people say improving your health in your bad times is helpful. Others say you must completely succumb to a health journey that levitates you and inevitably drops you into the category of healing where the metaverse decides you belong. You, my friends, must be the Plinko chip in your self-healing journey, so let's just see where you land.

There is a miniscule piece of truth in that, I believe. There is a kismet journey of linking arms with the right people, at the right time, in the right frame of mind, and with the right supports, where *all* the stars have aligned to match you to where you should ultimately be. Let's be real here... You cannot find meaning in everything around you.

The meaningful part comes in finding where you fit in it all. Where you can ultimately see yourself and your faults and revel in the disaster of it all. I believe, in the deepest parts of my heart and soul, that not only recognizing the messiness of life but actually reveling in it, squeezing the best parts of the mess through the cheesecloth of everyday life, leaves you with the absolute, gut-wrenching, real truth.

It can be ugly, but it is the truthful version. The version you never wanted to reveal, but secretly *always* wished someone would see. The human-first, grace-first, real version that every living being wants to embrace. That human experience in all of its complexity, which ultimately reflects back to yourself, is life's greatest gift and greatest lesson.

I have found that people are on different paths, which leaves me nowhere *near* being any sort of authority on the subject. What I do know, after decades of my experiences, is that the well-crafted and carefully curated people I have known over the years are the ones who fall the hardest. Those who push forward their fallacies and the tenderly offered examples of their humanity are what I can only describe as the antidote to the status quo. I am so ridiculously blessed with friends who nearly never hold themselves to an expectation of superficial perfection. For that, I often pinch myself, to be sure my friendship and relationship jackpot is real.

Here is my last-call definition of "health" in all its forms. It is a prescription that I *finally* am writing down right here and now, to be sure I can pass it on to others.

You are not perfect. I hate to break it to you, prince or princess, but it is the truth. You have heard it already (I am assuming) and maybe didn't want to believe it. But there you go. I know it is a shocker, but *you* are at fault sometimes. *You* are a total asshole sometimes, and for no good or profound reason. And this will happen a lot. You have made a "few" mistakes that are, hate to break it to you again, *your fault!* Let that resonate, land where it needs to. Own that real estate in yourself, because it is only *yours* to own!

Life will afford you opportunities to widen your perspective on all kinds of things. Take those opportunities and run with them. Go out and meet people whom you never thought you would meet. Take their experiences, emotions, and memories, and absorb them into yourself, appreciate them. Do not make them your own, but use them to broaden your perspective. Maybe take a second to look at your life and that of other people around you through a different lens, without judgment and with eyes wide open.

Learn about *others*! Although it is easy to feel misunderstood, which inevitably plants seeds of distrust and apathy toward others, please, don't be *that* person. Seriously, just don't. The world—hell, even your own town has flooded our streets with indignant, entitled, and self-righteous people who have a bone to pick with everyone. Don't volunteer to bury that bone for them.

Not responding to things that are the equivalent of emotional clickbait *is* a response. Not every situation, good, bad, or otherwise, requires you to throw your hat into the ring. I have had these conversations with my sons repeatedly. Sometimes, silence and not engaging in the subtle (and sometimes not-so-subtle) stabs at you show your strength in character.

However, stand firm in your resolve, and do not be afraid to stand up or to protect yourself and those whom you love. It has been incredibly liberating for me to show up in a way that requires others to respect me, my voice, and my truth. A skill that I didn't know I had until recently.

I like to think about all my own "empty cups." I do have empty cups that I leave all over my house. I like to think of it as my trail of breadcrumbs that maps out my own ADHD brain, which I live with each day. I forget why I walk into almost any room, *almost* every day. I have heard this type of thinking is the equivalent of keeping forty-seven tabs open in your internal browser, each half-finished, and eventually throwing it all down the toilet and starting all over the next day and the next and the next.

This thing is something I have tried to medicate at times, but it just requires a little more diligence on my part and being honest with myself to manage it. I see this in so many people, especially in the women in my life. I think it happens to be much more prevalent and real with women of my age. This got me thinking that maybe it is because of the expectation that women can *only* function daily with forty-seven tabs open, constantly. Perhaps, women just believe they may will likely fail miserably, if they don't keep those tabs open simultaneously, all of the time. For me, I am guilty as charged.

Also, on my personal proverbial rap sheet, I plead guilty to becoming a people pleaser, an ignorer, a blind follower, a friendship fixer, a problem fixer, and an unlicensed dumping ground of problems that never belonged to me. I don't know exactly when it started. Maybe I watched my mother help too many people in her career and watched my dad try to help and sponsor anonymous addicts, so that he slowly disappeared from our own family. I watched others in my family take on careers where they are helping others. There just were never any healthy limits for me as to how much I would choose to pour out to other people. I considered my being this way was just who I was, good, bad, or otherwise.

Why the hell did it take me so long to figure out that, while it may feel noble and (for me) utterly necessary to take these things on, it *isn't* noble at all. It's shoving your own desires, needs, and health (in all its forms) down the garbage disposal. When you have to live your life with this lovely pair of qualities, being a people-pleaser with

ADHD, sometimes I catch myself thinking, "Wait, who am I fixing or pleasing today?" And then it starts all over the next day and the next day and the next.

I used to take inventory each evening of what I forgot to do for my children, my husband, my home, and my job. All the while, my kids would gently retreat and watch their crazed mother flounder about. Yet, this is the expectation of parents and definitely of women in general. Do not mistake this for any kind of pity party—because *that* is bullshit. This is also why my chosen family, my true and genuine friends, have all expressed how this level of expectation is making women sick. Making them sick both inside and out.

Maybe we can shove that expectation full of alcohol, medications, perhaps CrossFit or yoga or maybe even food. But ultimately, I think you can come to the same conclusion each time. It is all bullshit.

I distinctly remember a conversation with my friend Marie where I was discussing yet *another* exhausting phone call with someone who had proceeded to drop yet *another* atomic bomb on my doorstep—again—with the expectation that I would be the one to talk it through, that I would be the one to absorb their pain and problems, and I would be passed the baton of ownership of said problem.

I explained what had happened and how I was frustrated and angry. Marie bluntly asked why these bombs land on my doorstep out of the blue, and why couldn't I just be left alone. She rarely handles these types of situations with kid gloves and basically said to me, "What the fuck, Erin? When is this going to stop?"

And then I realized that I was guilty, as well. What I really was looking to do was to pass on that baton to anyone else whom I could give it to, instead of stopping the bullshit cycle of owning everything that didn't belong to me.

Slowly, my children watched me deteriorate by the end of each day, filled with anger that "nothing was getting done." But how could it? The veil of perfection had become my wet blanket by 3:30 in the afternoon, and I was too busy trying to fix everyone else's problems, instead of admitting I had myriad problems of my own.

All the while, we had hit the five-year mark of the woman from my husband's affair's still continuing to work for our company. Mind you, I had bent my heart into two, trying to be stoic, strong, and permissive, and continuing with my second conviction listed above, being a professional ignorer. I would tell my closest friends that it didn't bother me that she continued to work for our company. I fully believed I could make a convincing argument to that effect. I was, however, an absolutely horrible liar. The situation with that woman had become my very own case of herpes. It would flare up at inopportune times and never, ever seem to go away.

And then, she did. She resigned from our company and left. I knew what my close confidants would say: It's about fucking time. They are, and were, absolutely 100% correct. Despite everything that would suggest otherwise to some people, that situation dragged my heart through the mud for five years.

Then a miraculous thing happened. It finally became my time to be myself. My time to finally end my own private parole sentence for my prior convictions. I'd paid all my dues; *all* of my restitution and then some. It took just a small amount of time, but I felt this unwinding, unclenching, massive exhale through my mind, my heart, my body, and my life.

It wasn't all daisies and sunshine. My body had held onto so much for so long, without any relief, that it only took a little nudge for the teetering tower of cards that was my life to crumble underneath me. I didn't know anything different than that edge I was constantly walking on. Finally, I could fucking breathe.

I think all people feel that friction, that intensity, that anxiety that things are just waiting to fall apart, and it *will* happen to a certain degree to everyone. It is just a matter of when. I can only speak for women, really, but women nowadays own so much more than they should. In truth, it just isn't a fair match. I decided I needed to start to rebuild myself, from the ground up.

Slowly, my health has improved, my heart has improved, my circle around me has shrunk, and my expectations of myself will be better than before.

So, let me reintroduce myself. My name is Erin, a recovering people pleaser, a recovering people fixer, a recovering friendship fixer, with boundaries that are currently under construction but almost complete.

I wish I could have seen all this sooner. I wish I could have known how great it feels to care more about yourself and less about things that do not belong on your plate.

I no longer pour myself into other people when my own cup is empty and I have nothing left to give. Even if there are cups in every room of my house, I won't apologize for them.

Moab Mishaps

I recently went to Moab, Utah with my son, his friends, and my husband. We have made this trip many times before. But for some reason, this trip felt different, probably because I was working on finally finishing this book.

To be truthful, every single trip we make as a family is always cause for extreme stress inside me, and therefore also residual stress for our family. Obviously, it is of my own making, because I often try to make everything perfect. I try to have things perfectly planned and executed. And yet, despite all of that, this trip ended almost disastrously.

The weather turned on us on our last day, as we tried to leave and head back home. The dried-up creek bed that was both the entrance and exit to our campsite had become a raging river of water and mud after a full night of heavy rain. While we knew the forecast mentioned the weather turning sour, we'd decided to stay one more night. As we have often said to ourselves before, we figured we'd be fine, we always are.

As we prepared to leave camp, we watched other cars and trucks in front of us end up completely stuck, with families panicking that they would not be able to get out. Frozen in fear. My husband and I quickly came up with a plan to get us out of there. It wouldn't be comfortable and would likely be freezing and difficult, but it was necessary.

Within two quick minutes, he and I were out of the car and removing excess weight from our fifth wheel camper, moving forward so we could try to make our attempt to leave. We looked at each other while all of the kids were in the back of our truck, and we knew it was risky. But we knew we had to try.

We gunned the truck with the fifth wheel attached, albeit with its lighter load, surging through the water that had slowly started to slow in the newly formed raging river within the muddy creek bed. I said a little prayer to myself and the kids in the back, and we blasted the truck straight through waist-high raging waters.

As the muddy water splashed up and over the sides of the truck, I remember thinking, "Erin, just keep going. Don't lose the momentum, or you will be washed away. Don't let fear stop you, and don't let the rain and mud keep us from getting to where we need to be. From where you *need* to be."

It didn't. We eventually were able to get out just fine, and we left Utah to return to Colorado as planned.

I thought long and hard about the weekend during the long drive back to Denver. Not just about our last day, but about the trip. I realized this was the first trip of this kind where my lack of planning didn't even matter. We were alive, healthy, and warm. We'd had a wonderful time, laughing and exploring off-road trails. We were all dirty—well, filthy, really. And on the drive home, we all talked about our adventures from the weekend and belly-laughed for hours.

After we returned, I spoke with a friend about the trip. She asked how it had gone, and I described our adventures, still giggling while we spoke about our mishaps. She mentioned that the trip sounded to her like a nightmare. I explained that, while it may sound that way, we *always* have some kind of adventure when we go away on trips like that. Really, we always seem to have adventures together.

To which she said she was glad I was laughing at all of it. Because she might have cried, if it were her. I said, "Why cry? There's always something to laugh about, no matter what." And that is what I wanted me, the kids, and my husband to take away from the trip.

It is simple to see where this is heading. The times in my life when I stopped trying to control the narrative, trying to do what is expected, and trying to be what I believed everyone else wanted me to be, have always ended in best of ways. Whenever I chastised myself for things going wrong, criticized and compared myself to other people, it always ended up as a self-fulfilling prophecy and, ultimately, felt like a disaster.

And those latter times always left me feeling like I'd made a mistake, failed, didn't make the cut, or didn't do something exactly right. They left a hole in my psyche that felt like it would never be filled. Good or bad, it just felt like I could never be truly whole or myself.

Here's the question I pose to you, whoever is reading this. Do you stay in that hole? Do you scrape the sides of that hole and continue the blaming and shaming of yourself? I guess you could potentially do that forever—I had always assumed I would.

But for me, that hole is no longer there. My shortcomings, if I even want to call them that, are attributes I am now truly grateful for. Doing what you can, when you can, the best that you can.

As for today's Afterschool Special (for those who even remember what those specials were), do you watch your kids watch *you*. Not the kind of watching you where they are waiting to see if you have discovered the naughty things they've already done. But when they are watching you intently, sort of drinking you into their soul.

My kids are getting older, which at times means they have little to no interest in me. But I can always tell when they are taking in and understanding what I am dishing out to them. That little spark in their eyes when I can tell they are really getting it, getting my message. Those moments are priceless.

I have talked with my kids throughout the years about their inner voices. How to "read a room" and how to show understanding, compassion, and empathy for others. In that process, I have also watched them choose to take the blame sometimes, even when they really should not have. Thankfully, that script has been flipped. It must be flipped.

Now that I am finally wrapping all of this up, I will leave you with these life lessons, which I feel I have learned the hard way:

* I have made mistakes—huge and little ones. I have felt shame, embarrassment, and insecurities about all of them. But I wouldn't change any of them for anything.

* None of the people I have ever met in my own life, ever, are or were perfect, either. That means their trajectory is undoubtedly similar to my own.

* Give grace when grace is due, but not when it is not due.

* Love those who love you *for* you, no matter what. Gross and disgusting faults and all.

* Thank your lucky stars that you woke up today, saw the sun, and hugged or kissed someone you love.

* Never, and I mean *ever*, think to yourself that what others expect of you is what you *should* do. It just may be exactly the opposite for you, and that is the wonderful tapestry of this life. It certainly has been for me.

Until next time, my friends...

Acknowledgments

I am so immensely grateful for this experience, and I want to thank the many different people and things that went into writing this book. How lucky can one girl get, to have more people than she even knew she would have to thank? I mean, wow.

Mom: for raising me to be myself, in all of my quirky forms, and for showing me how to be a mom, too. You are a marvelous human being, a loving grandmother, a wise woman, a risk-taker, and the strongest woman I have ever met. I have watched you weather unbelievable storms, experiences, and circumstances with grace, just like your own mom and her mom before her. As your mom told you, and as you have told me, we come by it honestly.

Dad: for loving me unconditionally. Even when sometimes I cannot see the good in me, you see the better in me and in my own gifts. You have been so humbly honest and kind to me. I would like to think my own creative spark and my artistic need for self-expression comes from the Johnson side of the family. Love you, Dad.

My brother: for showing me and the world that people are not always what they seem to be. And that people may have the potential to do something just amazingly unexpected with their lives. You are a funny, incredibly smart, disciplined, and, most important, the most incredible dad and husband to your family. I've said this before, but I am so grateful to be navigating this adult world with a sibling. Without you, it would be lonely as hell, and who would I make inside jokes with about our childhood? I love you, big brother.

And on another note, here is my friendship gratitude roll call:

E. M.: for being the absolute best BFF/sounding board who is and has been always there for me. Always. You are my hilarious, witty, intelligent, kind, loving, gorgeous, and steadfast friend. You keep me in touch with the world, with humor, with style, with music, with adventures, and have demonstrated what an honest lifelong friendship is. Man, what would I do without you in my life? My boys are the luckiest of young men to have you as their amazing auntie.

M. A.: for testing the boundaries of how I viewed friendship. *Ooof.* You started as someone who terrified me and ended up being the person who is my soft-landing spot, when I need it. Despite the awful experiences we have had together, I would like to think we are, today, the women we never thought we could be. I am so grateful you came into my life and let me jump into your own battles. It gave me the purpose I didn't even know I needed at the time. I love you. But I love Tilly and Gus more.

M. G.: for walking hand-in-hand with me through this journey with nothing but love, patience, grace, and friendship. You never let me fall too far and are always willing to help pick me up with your nuggets of spirit and wisdom. You were put into my life in the strangest and wildest of ways, but I could not be more grateful that it happened.

C. P.: for being my partner in crime over the years, my keeping-it-real friend, and someone who has watched me walk the path of growing up and parenthood and then followed suit. I love our memories, the debauchery we experienced together, and the private jokes from our crazy lives and history together. And let's be honest, you keep my hair looking amazing—something often envied by strangers. You are so amazing at what you do, and I am not just talking about hair. I am so very proud of what you have done with all your gifts. I love you more than you will ever know.

J. S.: for being a ride-or-die friend and part of the mom brigade I met right when I really needed them in my life. I am eternally grateful that we can now look forward to being irresponsible parents of adults. I fully see and expect you to soon be living your best life on a beach somewhere soon. Love you, friend.

H. B.: for being another member of my mom brigade. When my kids began school as little ones, I wish someone would have explained how important it is to find your own mom tribe. You offer such love, support, humor, and insight and show me what it is like to have your shit together as a mom. Dear God, I need that so much and love our girls' trips, too. I sure love our shared parenting experiences, and you.

K. S.: First, for introducing me to my now husband, way back when. I know we were up to no good for much of our childhood together, but you are such an integral part of who I am today. And if I recall that correctly, it goes all the way back to swim team? Nonetheless, I am so very grateful we held onto our friendship over these years. You are a true gem. A hilarious, smart, beautiful, and insightful gem. This world is a brighter place with you in it.

And for the key players...

To Samantha Joy: I don't know what I did to deserve you. The universe connected me to you in a strange and roundabout way, but apparently for the best of reasons. I will never be able to express how grateful I am that it did. Thank you for listening to me ramble, for not giving up on me when I was certainly ready to quit, and for helping me work through the wounds that opened during this writing process, ones I didn't even know I needed to heal. Most importantly for kindly and gently walking me through this process of writing a book. To put it mildly, this experience has thoroughly changed my life, and I cannot wait to see where it leads from here. You are a marvel, and I consider myself lucky to have had your help and guidance through this process. Here's to hopefully more books together!

To Kathryn: For helping me make sense of my thoughts and for hopefully making them sensible to everyone else.

To Andy: for making me look and feel beautiful, and for helping me come out of my shell. I was able to show my true self on the outside as well as on the inside.

To Tamara: for listening to me, guiding me, and helping me walk through some incredibly dark and scary *times.* I believe you also allowed me to be the reason that *you* go to therapy.

To Gillian Flynn, Liane Moriarty, Glennon Doyle, Paula Hawkins, Kurt Vonnegut, Delia Owens, Lisa Jewell, Brené Brown, and Jessica Knoll: Thanks for making art through your writing that lives on in different parts of my heart and soul.

To New Order, Depeche Mode, The Cure, Sade, Sisters of Mercy, James, The Stone Roses, Nitzer Ebb, Fleetwood Mac, Miike Snow, George Michael, White Lies, The Cult, Drake, Pat Benatar, Lana Del Rey, Maxwell, Prince, Kacey Musgraves, LCD Soundsystem, Jody Watley, Banks, Kool & The Gang, and, dare I say, Taylor Swift: You helped this woman navigate her ups, downs, break-ups, make-ups, friendships, and family throughout my time on this Earth so far. There aren't enough thank-yous for your contributions to sparking creativity and seemingly endless adventures in my life.

To my kids: You will never know how much I love you. Ever. You bring so much life to my own life and continue to show me your kindness toward each other and other people. This makes my heart overflow constantly. Even more than that, I get you both, and I adore your personalities and who you both are. This makes me even more confident in who you will both inevitably become. You are both, at your cores, good human beings, and that makes me so crazy proud of you both. I really hope you both see this book as something to be proud of, too.

Lastly, to my husband: From where we started, where we went, and where we are, it takes my breath away.

When I look at our life together now, I know it has been a long road of the best and the hardest decisions and experiences we have both shared. This writing process has been a journey for you, too. But you are my lobster, and you will always be my lobster. I am so proud of us. The proudest I have ever been in my life. I know we have so much more to do together in this life, and I cannot wait.

About the Author

Erin Hunt was born in Dickinson, North Dakota but raised primarily in the beautiful state of Colorado, where she still lives and works. She considers her family, friends, and health to be most important thing to her. After over fifteen years working in law, corrections, treatment, and social work, and after her thirty-three-year relationship and eventual marriage, Erin has decided to share her story and memories.

When she isn't spending time with her friends and family, you can almost always find her surrounded by her French bulldogs, Chanel and Jules. *Lovely Disaster* is Erin's first book.

www.ingramcontent.com/pod-product-compliance
Lightning Source LLC
Chambersburg PA
CBHW031158270326
41931CB00006B/324